# BIKE.
# CAMP.
# COOK.

*A smooth mountain road in Sicily*

# BIKE. CAMP. COOK.

The Hungry Cycle Tourist's Guide to Slowing Down, Eating Well, and Savoring Life on the Open Road.

## Tara Alan

Going Slowly, LLC
Arlington, Vermont

Copyright © 2013 by Tara Alan
Photographs copyright © 2013 by Tara Alan & Tyler Kellen

All rights reserved. This book or any portion thereof may not be reproduced or used in any manner whatsoever without the express written permission of the publisher except for the use of brief quotations in a book review.

Printed in the United States of America

First Printing, 2013

ISBN 978-0-615-87833-1
PCN 2013949324

Published by Going Slowly, LLC
Arlington, Vermont
http://www.goingslowly.com

Photography by Tara Alan & Tyler Kellen
Edited by Tara Alan & Tyler Kellen
Cover design & illustrations by Megan Blondeau
Going Slowly logo by Alex Blondeau

Blackberries ripening near a free-camp in Italy

The view from our tent at a campsite in France

## Acknowledgements

**Megan**, my dear friend and designer extraordinaire, thank you so much for generously donating your time and expertise to this project. Your thoughtful additions have made this book a million times better than I could have ever hoped for.

**Jodi**, thank you for letting me hijack your kitchen for months on end, labeling all of the food in the house with notes like, "For BOOK purposes ONLY! Do not eat!" So many people have mother-in-law horror stories, but I think I hit the jackpot when I married Tyler and you became my Jodi-in-law. Thank you for your support, and especially for your enthusiasm. I love you.

**Mom, Dad, and Lian**, I feel so privileged to have been born into such a loving, supportive family. I often find myself in grateful awe of your complete and utter belief in my abilities (even when I remain doubtful), your enthusiasm about my many adventures (even when they are unconventional), and your willingness to always lend a hand. Your unconditional support has always lifted me up. I love you all so, so much.

**Grandma Jeanne**, I feel inordinately lucky that during the process of writing this book, I've been spending more time with you than ever before. I cherish the fact that I can have a relationship with you as an adult—you bring so much joy to my life. Thank you for being so enthusiastic about this book, and so eager to read what I've written. I love you dearly.

**Many thanks** to Grandma & Grandpa Cohen, Dan & Julia, Mary & Jack, and Jess, Nick, Pete, and Natasha. Thank you to all the nice people we met on the road, and to all the friendly folks who followed our journey online. Lastly, THANK YOU to all of you wonderful Kickstarter backers (featured on the following pages) who helped turn this book into a physical reality. We did it!

# To my generous team of Kickstarter backers:

Aaron
Adam Carpenter
Adam Townsend
Addison & Jahnavi (The Love Sprockets)
Aileen Elliot
Alan Harper
Alastair Humphreys
Alberto
Alexandre Dumontet
Alex & Megan Blondeau
Alex Thompson
Ali Stewart & Erik Dellea
Alice Simpkins
Alicia Ackerman
Alicja Szajerka
Amie Thao & Olli Tumelius
Amy Smidutz
Andrea
Andrea Aeschlimann & Bruce Mabbott
Andreas Straub
Andrée & David Bazinet
Andrew
Andrew & Crystal Bailey
Andrew Livingston
Andrew Szeto
Andy Schmid
Angel Barclay & Austin McKimmey
Angie
Ania & Robb Maciag
Anne Struffert
Anthony Green Buffet
April Arroyo
April Luokkala
Ashley Steigerwalt
Barbara Wachs
Bartłomiej Sosna
Bartosz Podlejski
Bay Area Bicycle Law
Beatrice Burton & Tucker Morris
@beau
Ben Davenport
Ben Parrilla & Eve Juarez
Beverly Scarboro Willingham
Bev Taylor
Bill
Bob
Bobbi Hardy
Bob & Jeanie Ransom
Boson Au-Perkins
Brandon Tinianov
Breanna Sheahan
Brenda Halfao
Brian Labuda
Brian Logan

Brian P. McCarty
Cara Hills
Caroline Kulesza
Cary & Sheila Stoffels
Casey
Cassidy & Lila
C. D. & Freda Barrington
Celeste LeCompte
Chandler & Jenny Engel
Charlie Lotte
Chas & Becky Moore
Cheryl & Martin Sunstrum
Chris
Chris Bernardi
Chris Goodman
Chris Reynolds
Chris & Sherry Allen
Christian
Cindy Mello
Cindy & Oscar Lepeley
Cis O'Boyle & Rachel Ferriman
Claire & John
Clélie D. D. Steckel
"Cowboy" Ben Alman
Cyndy
Dale Nick
Dan & Jennifer Grant
Danell Lynn (2 Wheeled Wanderlust)
Danika
Dan & Manu - Better Life Cycle
Danny Sanchez
Dare
Darrell & Deb
Darsha Hardy
Dave
Dave Beachley
David Bickerstaff
David Cox
David & Jen
David Morton
David Nichols
David Ramirez
David Seipel
Dean Campbell
Debbie Black
Deb Schumacher
Dell
Demetra Gates Choi
Dennis Kleine
Derric P.
Didier Jourdain
Dirk
Donna Sakson
Drew W.
Dylan Glynn
Eddo

Elizabeth
Elizabeth & Weez
Eliza Hudson & Jamestowne Cliff
Elle Bustamante
Ellen Lofaro
Emily Bruce
Emily Crocker
Emma C.
Emma & Justin Logan
Emma & Matt
Eric Portis
Erin
Ernest Allred
Evelyn & Mary
Frank de Neling & Dagmar Hekelaar
Frank Morris
Franny & Hannes
Fred Juengling
Frodosghost
George Hetrick
George Mandis
Gérald Berthier
Gio
Grandma Jeanne
Greer Hogan Kobik
Greg
Greg Morris
Greg Scott
Greta & Jesse
Guntawee Tiwapong
Guy & Freddie (ABikeJourney.com)
Haidee & Rob Thomson
Heather
Heather Drummond
Heather & Luke
Helen Dowson
Helen Marshall
Holly Aitchison
Iain D Crawford
Ian!
Ian Breckheimer
Ian Cook
I. Kind
Isaac Frerichw
Isabel F
Jack Gross & SUS '12
Jacqueline Campbell
Jacqui
Jakub K.
James Lambie
Jan
Janelle & Ryan Chism
Jane Mountain
Jane Nosal & Bob Samway
Jane Richter
Janet & Jay

Janice Rutherford
Jared & Rachel Pardi
Jason Amdor
Jason Koning
Jason Vargas
Jasper J. Kort
Jay Adriaanse
Jean Blondeau
Jed Bowtell
Jeff
Jeff Aurand
Jeff "the chef" Mika
Jen Comiskey
Jenna
Jennifer Gunji-Ballsrud
Jennifer Iversen-Curry
Jennifer McPhie
Jenni Whicker
Jenny & Matthew
Jenny Stratton
Jill Sible
Jim Boswell
Jim Carson
Jim & Diane Omans
Jim Hood
Joan
Joanna & Greg Tebbano
JoAnne
Joanne Ottaway & David Grosshans
JodiMama
Joe Comiskey
Joe Lionnet
Joe Richier
John Garvey
John Kerry O'Sullivan
Johnny
Jon Null
Jonas Atterbring
Jordan, Macklin, & Gretchen's Dad
Josephine Lee
Joshua Redfearn
Julia E.T. Hood
Julianno Francisco
Julie Birdwell
Julie McLean
Jumanji
Jurjan Dijkstra
Justina Block
Justin Bruno
Justin Davis
Kaitie Worobec
Kaitlin
Kale Brewer
K.A. Moylan
Karina "Beana" Lepeley & Ivica Cvetkovic
Kate

Kate Roper & Andy Thomas
Kathleen Katie L. Morris
Katie Taylor
Katrina
Katy Manar Fechter
Kaylin Bradley
Keeshia Barker
Kelly Stahl
Ken
Ken Flor
Ken & Jocelyn deBoer
Ken Kobayashi
Kenneth Tse
Kenn Martin
Kevin Goodall
Kevin & Joy O'Brien
Kevin & Marion
Kevin T. Miller
Kim Christiansen
Kjartan Holmen
Kris Engeman
Kurt A Schneider
Lane Christiansen
Lara Dossett
Laurent Lebecque
Leo M. Schwaiger
Liam James Leaven
Lian Reggie Alan
Lily Moselle
Linda Flach Corl & Terry Corl
Linda L.
Linda Linssen
Linda, Phil & Luca
Lisa
Lisa B.
Lisa & Mark Alan
Lisa Micele
Lisa & Phil Graff
Lloyd
Lloyd & Vinny Gaby NZ
Ludmila
Magalie L'Abbé & Travis Rathert
Magdalena Dudek
Magdalena Hutter
Malcolm Dodds
Mandy Noonan
Manjula Martin
Marc Salonsky
Marcin Jankowski
Marek Miloszewski
Margaret
Marilee Tuohy
Mark Foley
Mark Porczak
Mark Rogerson
Martina Gees, Colorfish
Martin Yeates
Marty
Marya Figueroa
Mary Niedenfuer

Mathias Kuhring
Matteo
Matthew Eagar
Matthew Shanahan
Matthieu Calu
Matt Irwin
Matt Koulermos
Matt Salisbury
Maxime Lachance
Maxim Nazarov & Polina Sporysheva
Mee Thao
Megan
Meizi Mao
Mel
Melissa Lovell
Menno
Mia & Matias
Michael Hammer
Michael Mann
Michael Tyson & Katherine Herriman
Michael Wade
Michal Brzozowski
Michelle Descoteaux
Mike Brown
Mike & Eliza
Mike & Marilyn
Mike Stoll
Mikolaj "MDikkii" Demków
Milestonerides.com
Mimi Connell-Lay
M. Tadashi Havey
Murph Kinney
Nadine Assfalg & Felix Heinrich
Nancy Kane
Nancy Peterson & Dave Ertel
Nan & Dave
Nan Woodbury & Gary Hochgraf
Naomi Asselin
Natalia Oprowska
Natalie Ceperley
Natasha Scheuerman & Peter Bryan
Nate Perry
Nate Simpson
Nick
Nick & Jess
Nicky Robinson
Nicolas Vandemaele-Couchy
Nicole
Nomadiclas
Oanh & Nic
Pamela Almoustine Bradford
Patricia Harrow
Patty & Mark
Paul Jackson

Paul Kennedy
Paul W. Dorr
Penelope
Pete Appleyard
Peter Gostelow
Phil Cluff
Philip Lomax
Phil, Kathy & Matthew
Poppy Calder
Rachel Tyson
Raj Taran Dev Arathi Shekhat
Randall
Ray Peregrino
Rebecca Hogue
Rebecca & Oshin Jennings
Rhian Roberts
Richard Ragle
Rik & Paula
Rob & Neisha Sanderson
Roberta Connelly
Rob Harkey
Rob Harrison AIA
Robin, Linnea, Amy & Peter
Rob & Juliette Prouse
Rob Kazmierski
Rob Roy
Rob Shaw
rodadas.net
Rompson Rally
Ron
Ronald van Eede
Russ
R. Walker
Ryan Kim
Sally Bruckert
Sally Waters
Sampsa Kotajärvi
Sam Tew
Samuel Joslin
Sandra Brakstad
Sarah Botzek
Sarah S
Sarah Tasto
Sarah Welle
Sarah "Yummy" Cooke
Scott Fraser
Scott Spearman
Sean Head
Severin Baron
Shannon Compton & Jon Wood
Share The Road Bicycle Tours
Sheila (2cycle2gether.com)
Sheila Truett
Sherry Dire
Simon
Simon Hart

SK Tan
smudgersambacycle.org
Song Hia
Stacey Caulk
Stacy Manalastas
Stefan Bauer
Steve
Steve Gibbins
Steve Proctor
Steve Woodside
Strawberry Fields
Suni Dixon & Willy Suen
Sunil Doshi
Tambra & Dan
Tandem Longhurst
Tara Kenny
The Bike Project of Urbana-Champaign
The Bruce Family
The Fineout Family
The Hoff Family
The Maple Hill Hood Neighbors
The Warnocks
Thomas Burleson
Thomas Dalmayrac
Thomas Paine & Diana Samour
Tim
Tim Collins - Do Something Epic
Tim Dyet
Tim Early
Tim Leary
Timothy Stark
Tim Scales
Tom Allen
Tom James
Tom Lehmann & Alexandra Sawyer
Tommaso Cecilia & baby Greta
Tom McHale
Tyler Kinnear
U ♥ J
University Laboratory High School Library
UT Outdoor Program & Lemon the Dog
Walnut Studiolo
Walt
Wander Cyclist
Wan Sophonpanich
Will Fulford-Jones
Yohann Paris
Yves & Ingrid (bikeaway.info)

**For Tyler**

Without your unflagging kindness and encouragement (not to mention your mischievous smile and incredible powers of persuasion), the me-back-then would never have decided to drop everything and travel around the world with you. It was you who showed me how to enjoy cycling, and you who opened my world to the great outdoors, and you who showed me that we could conquer any challenge we faced.

Without our (first) journey of a lifetime, the thought of making this book would never have popped into existence. More practically speaking, this book would have never happened without your consistent gentle prodding, your unwavering confidence in my abilities, your willingness to wash a thousand dishes, your razor-sharp bullsh*t-o-meter, your recipe testing prowess, your commitment to clarity and excellence, and your dedication to skillfully editing hundreds of rambling pages. Thank you, thank you, a thousand times thank you.

I love you.

*On April 1st of 2009, my partner Tyler and I left our home in Minnesota to embark on the adventure of a lifetime. It was our first-ever bicycle tour, an unsupported expedition from Scotland to Southeast Asia, spanning two years and twenty-five countries. We pedaled our way across Western Europe, spent a winter in Tunisia, cycled across Eastern Europe, bought a car and drove across Russia and Mongolia, and finished with six months of cycling in Southeast Asia. We wrote about the adventure daily on our website, goingslowly.com. The experience changed the trajectory of our lives forever.*

Asia

Our tent pitched in a flowery German field

# PART ONE: GETTING READY

Introduction  16

The Pedal-Powered Pantry  23

In the Camp Kitchen  69

# PART TWO: THE RECIPES

Breakfast & 2nd Breakfast  101

Lunch & Snacks  131

The Suppertime Feast  163

Desserts  237

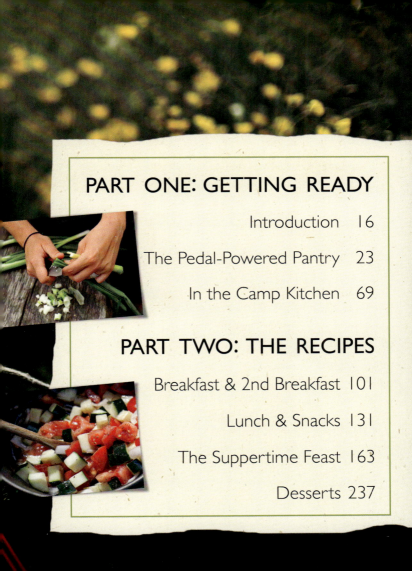

Waking up in our dewy tent in Italy

# PART ONE: GETTING READY

# INTRODUCTION

This book was born within the rustling nylon walls of our trusty tent, pitched on a grassy hill in the outskirts of Rome. Four months into our two-year journey across Europe and Asia, I was inspired by a particularly delicious meal I'd made. So, I opened a text file on my laptop, named it "Recipes for the Road," and began to type.

As a completely inexperienced bicycle tourist, I had embarked on our journey under the assumption that my love of cooking would continue on the road. I was blithely unaware, for example, that it was common practice for adventurers to eschew cooking altogether, instead subsisting on such dismal fare as plain bread, rapidly-rotting bananas, and anything prepared with boiling water alone.

My logic was simple: because we cooked our meals from scratch at home, we would be cooking our meals from scratch on the road. With that in mind, I created a rolling kitchen that churned out gourmet food nearly every day. After several months of traveling, I was beginning to feel that I had something to share with the bicycle touring community.

That night, my fingers tap-danced across the keyboard, scarcely able to hold pace with my stream of consciousness. I wrote about how I organized food and cooking tools in our panniers, and which groceries yielded the most options for a variety of meals. I talked about how we used our hot pasta water to soak dirty dishes, and how we got by without refrigeration, an oven, or a well-stocked grocery store.

And I wrote, of course, about the food I'd made: the potato leek soup I concocted on our first night in chilly Scotland, and the garlicky, cheesy pasta that had become Tyler's go-to favorite. I wrote about the vegetable stir-fries, the homemade chicken strips, and the soups made from wild, foraged sorrel. I wrote about our standard breakfast of buttery crepes, and how to make rice puddings that tasted like heaven. Eventually, hours later, I saved my work, shut my computer, and called it a night.

It would be several years before I would open that file again. With our bicycle tour behind us, we settled into a more stationary lifestyle, and I decided to devote some time to the creation of a bicycle touring cookbook. This is that creation.

I daydream about food constantly, especially when I'm on my bicycle. As I pedal, my mind is endlessly churning through culinary possibilities, generating ideas for camp-friendly meals. My hope is that this book will channel that never-ending stream of cooking inspiration, diverting as much of it as possible straight to you.

Nearly everything I've learned about cooking on the road over the course of two years has been condensed within these pages. So, whether you're a bicycle tourist who knows little about cooking, or a foodie who is unwilling to sacrifice good eats for an adventure on the open road, you'll find something of value here.

We'll start with the basics—what to pack and how to fit it in your panniers. We'll chat about collecting spices, filling your fuel bottle, and carrying water, along with many other topics that will help you get started on the path towards preparing gourmet camp meals. Then, with the foundation in place, we'll get cooking!

The recipes in this book are a mixture of my favorite things to cook on the road, and a number of dishes that I developed after we returned from our journey. They were created with the adventurous, food-loving, traveling cyclist in mind—you won't need a refrigerator, freezer, or oven to make them. Some of the recipes are ridiculously simple, while others involve multiple steps, a few dirty bowls, and a lot of pizazz.

It is my hope that this book will make cooking on the road a fun and rewarding activity, instead of a dreaded chore to be avoided. If you don't have the energy to prepare a satisfying meal at the end of a riding day, maybe, just maybe, you're cycling too far or too fast. This book is an invitation to *slow down* and smell the wild garlic. It's an invitation to revel in the celebration of food that is camp cuisine. Flavor need not be sacrificed at the altar of hardcore adventure. When you taste your first bite of tomato mozzarella calzone (page 229) or cherry chocolate turnover (page 242), you'll understand just what I'm talking about.

With this book as your guide, expect to have a lot of fun, make a bunch of messes, dirty a zillion dishes, and taste some of the best meals you've ever had on tour. Before long, you'll have people coming to your campsite, lured in by the aroma of your outdoor kitchen, exclaiming "you eat better out here than I do at home!"

*Cooking supper by headlamp light in Greece*

*Preparing to make soup in the "Bike.Camp.Cook.Test Kitchen"*

# THE PEDAL-POWERED PANTRY

# COOKING EQUIPMENT & BASIC TOOLS

Before you embark on a culinary journey towards creating fantastic camp meals, you're going to need some basic cooking tools. The items I discuss on the following pages form the foundation of my traveling kitchen; I've used each of them over a thousand times.

Not all of these tools are indispensable, but each of them will definitely make the act of preparing delicious meals on the road as pleasant and stress-free as possible. With that in mind, here are my essentials, in no particular order:

### *A non-stick cookset*
In the same way you want to pack a quality sleeping bag to ensure a good night's sleep, it's important to get a great cookset to help you prepare a delicious meal at the end of each day.

I have the GSI Pinnacle Backpacker. It's what Tyler and I used on our adventure, and it's what we used to test and re-test the recipes in this book dozens of times. It's not imperative that you use the same cookset, but please know that I've tailored the recipes to be made with one that has the following features:
- A 2-litre capacity **non-stick** pot
- An 8"/20.32cm **non-stick** frying-pan
- A sturdy lid, preferably with small holes on one side to be used for straining.
- A handle that fits securely. If your set only comes with one, be sure you can change it from pot to frying pan easily with one hand. Or, buy an extra so you have two.

As long as your cookset has these features (*the most important being the non-stick surface*), you'll be fine. If you're traveling solo, you can make half-batches of the recipes and use a slightly smaller pot, but I don't recommend going any smaller on the frying pan.

## *A camp stove & fuel bottle*

In addition to pots and pans, you'll need a stove. I have the most experience with MSR's Whisperlite International. After literally thousands of uses, I can recommend it wholeheartedly.

The Whisperlite International accepts all kinds of fuel, but I run mine solely on unleaded gasoline—it's the easiest and cheapest fuel to acquire around the world. It can be a bit sooty when priming, but I haven't found that to be a problem.

The Whisperlite is a notoriously powerful stove, and coaxing it to a low setting can be tricky. Many of the instructions in my recipes offer tips and guidance on how to deal with this. If you're a wizard with a Whisperlite, or if your stove has a wider range of temperatures (besides crazy hot and obscenely hot), you'll want to adjust your cooking technique accordingly.

In addition to the stove, I carry a 20oz MSR fuel bottle. When cooking every day, a bottle lasts about a week and costs less than a dollar at each fill-up. For advice on how to keep your bottle topped up, see page 26.

## *Wind Screen*

In order to make efficient use of your fuel, you'll want to use a wind screen. If your stove comes with a flimsy one like mine did, consider getting a more sturdy replacement. I like the kind that folds up accordion-style.

# AT THE FUEL STATION

If you've never rolled into a gas station on a gigantic bicycle, you've been missing out on one of the more amusing aspects of bicycle touring. Get ready for pointing, chuckling, and confounded expressions as people try to figure out why you could possibly need gasoline. Here's how to fill up with a minimum amount of fuss:

Fetch your fuel bottle from a pannier. If it's pressurized, open it slowly and take care to keep it away from your eyes—it might spray a little bit. Set the bottle on the ground, wedging it firmly between your feet. Then, stick the fuel nozzle (I use the lowest octane available) into the bottle and, as slowly as you can, squeeze the handle. It often sprays much faster than you'd like, and will bubble up for a minute, looking like it's full. It probably isn't. Give the fuel a moment to settle down, and then repeat the process until you've reached the fill line.

When you're done, screw on the fuel pump cap securely and wipe down the outside with a rag or paper towel. Double wrap the bottle in a plastic bag, and stow it away in a pannier. Pay, and roll out!

> In some countries, gas-pumping is done for you. In these cases, you may have to convince the worker that your fuel bottle is a legitimate container for gasoline. My advice is to be friendly, and to get good at miming "It's for cooking!"

## *Fire*

I carry a lighter (I've had enormous success finding perfectly good ones by the side of the road while riding), as well as a flint and steel. I recommend having at least two fire-starting implements with you at all times.

## *Cooking utensils*

I began touring with a set of fancy collapsible camp utensils, but to my dismay, almost all of them fell apart or melted in a matter of weeks. I replaced them with an inexpensive set of wooden spoons, and the smallest silicone spatula I could find. I've been a much happier cook ever since. To make the recipes in this book, you'll want to have the following:

- 1 simple wooden spoon
- 1 small silicone spatula
- A ladle, such as the MSR Alpine Spoon

## *Dishes*

I use collapsible Sea to Summit X-bowls, X-plates, and X-mugs. I like them because they pack up nicely, and because their flat, food-grade nylon bottoms double as cutting boards. I use them as much for food preparation as I do for eating. I recommend carrying at least:

- 1 8" plate with a lip
- 1 bowl per person
- 1 mug per person

## *Knives*

Good knives are indispensable. A sharp pocket knife works well for most on-the-road food prep, but I recommend bringing a larger fixed-blade as well. A bowie knife fits the bill, but I think that a small chef's knife would do the job even better. I haven't tested this theory yet, but if you give it a shot, let me know how it goes!

## Sporks

I carry a pair of lightweight Snow Peak titanium sporks and heartily recommend them for their durability and sleek design. They get bonus points for being crafted from reclaimed submarine parts!

## Cutting board

Unless your plates double as cutting boards, this will be your only working surface. With that in mind, make it a useful one. I loathe flimsy, flexible "camp" cutting boards. Instead, I carry a lime green plastic one that I bought ages ago at a department store. It slides nicely into the back pocket of my cooking pannier.

## Measuring spoons

Measuring spoons are small, light, and easily packable. Definitely bring them along so you can try all of the recipes in this book with successful results.

To be perfectly honest, I rarely measure anything while cooking, and *never* when I'm on the road. Instead, I trust my taste buds, instincts, and years of experience to guide me. If I could convey that first-hand knowledge to you, I would, but instead I've converted my "season to taste" attitude into a more quantifiable format for this book's recipes.

## A can opener

Bring the smallest and sturdiest one you can find. It doesn't need to come from a fancy outdoors store; any old thing will do, as long as it works.

## A vegetable peeler

I don't usually peel my vegetables before using them (I just can't be bothered), but this device is small, easily packable, and can be handy to have anyway.

*Various and sundry cooking tools and utensils*

### *Waterproof basin*

This is what you'll use as a sink when a traditional one isn't available. The case of my cookset doubles as a waterproof basin, and it works well as a place to wash small dishes or rinse vegetables. Some cycle tourists we know swear by their Ortlieb folding bowls. Whatever you choose, you'll be using it a lot, so bring a good one.

### *Assorted containers with excellent-fitting lids*

You'll be carrying many foods that will need a safe and secure home in your panniers, and thus, you'll want to have various containers in which to store them. To serve this purpose, I've used everything from dollar-store plastic containers to old glass salsa jars.

Whatever you use, *make sure it has a tight-fitting lid*. Put some water in your prospective container, shake it around, and see what happens. Does it leak? Does the lid come off? Would it be best to secure it with a rubber band? Would it be better suited to store dry food or wet food? What if it tips over?

Thinking about your containers in this way will help you minimize the chance of spills.

### *A long-handled scrubber & eco-friendly dish soap*

Readily available hot water can sometimes be hard to come by on the road, and since tackling greasy pots and pans with ice-cold water is more comfortable at a distance, bring a long-handled scrubber. As well, be good to your environment and try your best to find biodegradable dish soap to carry with you!

### *Water purification device*

Depending on the type of tour you're planning, you may need to carry iodine droplets, a reliable filter, or a UV light water purifier to render your water potable.

## *Three-legged stool*

Because I rarely camp in places that have picnic tables or chairs, I consider my three-legged stool to be indispensable for on-the-road cooking. I carry a Swedish-made "Walkstool" with telescoping legs. In the closed position, it's perfect for squatting comfortably while preparing ingredients or cooking. I cannot recommend it enough—it will make your life on the road so much more comfortable!

Little birds enjoy our stools too!

# STAPLE INGREDIENTS

I like to think of the food we eat on a bicycle tour as falling into two categories. First, there are fresh foods including fruits, vegetables, meats, and dairy products such as milk or yogurt. I purchase produce every couple of days, and meat and milk sparingly—only if I know I am going to prepare and eat them within a few hours.

The rest falls into the second category, that of staple ingredients: things like flour, grains, pasta, canned food, and spices. These are the workhorses of the cycling cook's pantry. They provide the backbone for your recipes, on top of which various fresh foods can be added.

Staple ingredients are also designated as such because of their long shelf life, which varies from several days to several months depending on the product. I include potatoes, onions, eggs, and hard cheeses in this category because, though they are technically fresh foods, I've found that they'll keep, unrefrigerated, for at least a week. On a bicycle tour where the pedaling cook usually lacks refrigeration, it's important to be well-stocked in foods that last.

On the following page begins a list of my favorite staple ingredients. Please note that I don't keep *all* of them in my pantry at all times. Instead, I rotate my supply depending on availability, what I feel like cooking, and how long things last. For example, I might choose to purchase a bag of rice when my oats run out, or I might devote a week to Asian recipes when I pick up a bottle of soy sauce.

## Salt

The recipes in this book are made with regular table salt, and that's all you really need to carry. If you've never tried any fancier salts though, I highly recommend branching out. There's a whole world full of new textures and flavors awaiting you, from charcoal-black lava salt to chunky crystals of pink Himalayan salt.

## Flour

I buy flour in the smallest quantity I can. In Europe, that means an adorable, tiny paper bag. In the United States, you'll probably be stuck with a massive, lumbering one. If you can, split it with a fellow traveler, or donate what you can't fit in your panniers to another grocery shopper.

If you manage to find a bulk flour bin, I recommend buying 2-3 cups at a time. That is a good amount to have on hand for the various ways I use flour in this book: it's the main ingredient in breakfast crepes, tortillas, calzones, and dumplings, and it's the thickening agent of soups and sauces.

If you store flour in the paper bag it comes in, you'll want to wrap it in a plastic bag to keep it from leaking. Moisture weakens the paper, which tears and splits in no time, leaving you with a mess to clean up. You can also ditch the paper entirely and store flour in one or two tight-sealing containers. I keep mine in a pair of plastic canisters I purchased for pennies at a discount store in England.

For the recipes in this book, you'll want regular, all-purpose flour. Organic and unbleached is best, but whatever is readily available in your part of the world will work just fine.

## *Sugar*

Even if you're not a fan of sugary foods, the smallest amount of sweetness can be used to balance tangy, acidic flavors. Sugar performs this task in several of my savory recipes. Whatever method you use to pack your flour (transferring to a container, or wrapping paper sacks in plastic) will work to prevent sugar leakage, too.

## *Potatoes*

Whether they're small and waxy, or gargantuan with a sandy, earth-colored exterior, potatoes are eminently versatile, and one of the most inexpensive foods to buy. I always have a few bouncing around in the bottom of a pannier, weight be damned. I keep them in a plastic bag, or simply leave them unwrapped. They last for ages, can take a beating, and can usually be salvaged even when they start to wrinkle and sprout.

## *Pasta*

I always keep a package or two of spaghetti, angel hair, or fettuccine standing upright in the back pocket of a pannier. It's comforting to know that if all else fails, I can fill my belly with pasta! All it takes is olive oil, salt, pepper, and a bit of garlic and chili flakes from your spice bag (page 47) to create a deliciously filling, dirt-cheap meal.

Once in a while, a package of shelf-stable Italian potato gnocchi will find its way into my panniers, making a convenient and delicious base for a myriad of sauces. With a cooking time less than half that of traditional pastas, these soft potato pillows make for a speedy and satisfying supper.

To vary things a little bit, I occasionally purchase a tangled brick of translucent rice noodles with which to cook Asian-inspired meals.

Potatoes in a Tunisian Market

### Rice

I occasionally carry rice (the real stuff, not Minute Rice), though I find it difficult to make a pot of fluffy steamed rice on the road. Instead, I like to cook it for ages until it practically melts, creating rice puddings (page 254) and risottos, both of which require very little effort or technical skill.

### Rolled oats (porridge oats)

They're light to carry, easily packaged in a bag or airtight container, and they make a simple and nutritious breakfast. Cook them into oatmeal (page 114), turn them into granola (page 103), or simply eat them raw with dried fruits, nuts, and a swirl of milk. Better yet, use them in one of my dessert recipes that calls for oats, such as chocolate fudge oat cookies (page 256).

American readers: try to buy oats in the bulk section of the grocery store so you don't have to figure out how to stuff a big red tube of them into your panniers. If the cardboard tube is all you can find, "re-pot" it (page 60) into a smaller container.

### Beans

I always have a can or two of beans tucked away in my rolling pantry. They're fantastic to have on hand for hearty soups and stews, dips and salads, or for a simple meal of rice and beans spiced with cumin and onion.

### Fresh onions

You can always find a few of these rolling around with the potatoes at the bottom of a pannier. I'm not sure I could stomach cooking without their spicy bite. They stay fresh for ages, but be sure to keep tabs on them—they'll eventually decompose in the dark underbelly of your pannier.

### Fresh garlic

Along with fresh onion, garlic is the basis of nearly all of my favorite savory recipes, and is one of my most beloved friends in the kitchen. I'm not sure if there's a better smell in the world than garlic sautéed in butter!

### Olive oil

I always carry a bottle of olive oil in one of my panniers. It stands vertically next to my cookset and gets used nearly every day in practically everything I make.

### Tomato paste

Little cans of tomato paste are easy to carry, highly concentrated, and incredibly versatile. With just a tin or two, you can make tomato soup (page 176), chili con carne (page 164), marinara sauce (page 194), and any other tomatoey dish you can imagine.

While 4-ounce cans are readily available in the United States and abroad, metal squeeze-tubes of tomato paste and other concentrated sauces and condiments are popular across Europe.

### Prepared pesto

I don't include a recipe involving pesto in this book, but I like to buy a jar now and then to keep on hand for a quick and easy pasta dinner. Simply cook the pasta, dump on the sauce, top with cheese if you've got any (asiago and parmesan are nice), and call it good.

### Ketchup

Packed with preservatives, this condiment keeps unrefrigerated just long enough for me to finish a small bottle. I use it to jazz up fried potatoes, or to create a sauce for Berlin-style *currywurst* (page 205). As always, buy a small amount, and toss it if it smells or tastes funky.

## *A lemon, lime, or a small bottle of vinegar*

Often, some acidity is needed to really make a meal shine. I use lemon or lime juice when cooking fruit, and I use some sort of vinegar for salad dressings (though you could also go with lemon juice). Balsamic is thick and sweet, and is my favorite for salads, but red-wine, white-wine, or apple cider vinegars are all good too.

There's no need to have *all* of these acidic elements on hand at once. Instead, vary your supply from time to time according to what you feel like making and what's available.

## *Soy sauce*

I carry soy sauce for Asian-inspired recipes, such as rice noodles with stir-fried broccoli and onion (page 190), soy peanut cabbage slaw (page 142), and sweet-spicy peanut noodles (page 197).

Despite recommendations for refrigeration, I've noticed that street vendors in Southeast Asia leave theirs out in warm weather all the time. When you purchase yours, be sure to buy one with a good sturdy cap and store it upright, wrapped in a plastic bag.

## *Peanut butter*

Your usage of peanut butter will probably depend on where in the world you're traveling, and where in the world you call home. Coming from the United States, peanut butter is a beloved staple for me.

If you can find it, try carrying a jar with you. Not only will you be able to fix yourself a quick peanut butter sandwich, but you'll also be able to create delectable sweet-spicy peanut noodles (page 197), and batches of chocolate fudge oat cookies (page 256) among many other treats.

## Dried fruit & nuts

Raisins, dried cranberries, and dried cherries, along with almonds, peanuts, walnuts, and pecans, make great staple snack foods. If you don't gobble them up plain or in recipes like granola bar bites (page 156), they'll keep unrefrigerated pretty much indefinitely.

## Evaporated milk, coconut milk, or UHT milk

Fresh milk doesn't keep long without refrigeration, but I have found small, juice-box sized cardboard cartons of UHT (ultra-heat treated) milk that can stay unrefrigerated for months, if not years.

Evaporated milk (not to be confused with sweetened condensed milk) is often found in the baking section of a supermarket, and is another easily transportable dairy product. It works well in recipes that call for regular milk or cream.

For a creamy dairy alternative, try a carrying a can or two of coconut milk, if you can find it. It's fantastic for simple curries like my carrot, potato, and pea curry (page 169).

## Jam

Whatever the fruit, you can't go wrong carrying a jar of jam along with you. If you're feeling adventurous, or if you find yourself with some battered, mealy fruit, try your hand at making your own (page 118).

## Eggs

Oh how I love eggs! They're tasty, full of good nutrients, and really handy to have around for many dishes, both sweet and savory. Try to find farm-fresh eggs from happy hens, and use "large" ones in the recipes. For more information, including how to carry them safely, see page 104.

## *Butter*

Unless you're cycling in a cold climate, your butter will probably go through a regular cycle of softening during the day and hardening at night. I recommend keeping butter in a leak-proof container to prevent oily spills; wrapping that container in a plastic bag will keep you even more protected. If you can't find butter in your part of the world (you poor thing), try using olive or coconut oil instead.

## *Cheese*

Cheese will last a surprisingly long time. If it becomes spotted with mold, you can usually salvage it by slicing off the bad bits. Hard cheeses like Parmesan keep better than softer varieties, and are wonderful shaved over pasta, or sliced thin for snacking with fresh vegetables. Slightly softer ones make great grilled cheese sandwiches (page 183), and any old cheese (or combination of several) will make a tasty pasta sauce (page 199).

Keep your cheeses in an airtight container, as the softer ones will get squishy in hot climates, and you don't want grease to seep all over your pannier.

## *Bread*

I always keep bread on hand for quick mid-day sandwiches (page 144) and simple grilled cheese suppers (page 183). It's useful at breakfast as well, as the foundation of one-eyed-sailors (page 106) and French toast (page 116).

## *Honey*

This sticky treat is great for drizzling over crepes (page 123), oatmeal (page 114), and thickly buttered bread. I'll often splurge on a large jar of local honey when I come across it, ignoring my rule about buying small.

### Chocolate

A bar of plain dark chocolate to gobble up after supper makes a great dessert, and I use chocolate as an ingredient in several recipes such as cherry chocolate turnovers (page 242), and chocolate fudge oat cookies (page 256). If Tyler and I had anticipated what chocoholics we would become on the road, we'd likely have tracked our consumption of the stuff, along with kilometers pedaled and number of countries visited!

### Cookies

It's nice to have something tasty, calorie-rich, and easily grabbable (like cookies!) to snack on while riding. They make great motivators as well; knowing there will be a chocolate-covered cookie at the top of the hill can make a hard climb a little more bearable!

### Emergency rations

It's important to have some "emergency rations" on hand in case you're low on food and shops are scarce. For me, this usually means the cheap, readily-available food of college students: ramen noodles. You can cook them into soup as intended, or, if you're really desperate, you can prepare them a simpler way: break the raw noodles into bite-sized chunks, place them in a bowl, and sprinkle on the flavoring powder. Enjoy this crunchy snack when there's nothing else to eat.

### The spice bag

In the next section of this book, I'll go into detail about what the spice bag is, and how it's used. But for now, all you need to know is this: it's the key to all camp-cooking. Never leave home without it!

📷 *A jam-packed Tunisian "superette"*

❗ The next time you go shopping for food, keep your eyes peeled for various and sundry packaged items that have a long shelf life. Do you see small cans of tuna, salmon, shrimp, or other fish products? How about tiny jars of Thai curry paste, Mediterranean olive paste, or sun-dried tomatoes? Always be ready to supplement your food supply with small, long-lasting packages of interesting edibles!

*Spices in the medina of Sousse, Tunisia*

Adding local flavors to your spice collection is one of the best parts about cooking on the road!

# THE SPICE BAG

Without question, the most important item in your stash of staple ingredients is the spice bag. It's light, easily packable, and it single-handedly makes your entire cooking-on-the-road operation possible. With a well-stocked spice bag, you'll be capable of turning even the most dire set of mini-market finds into something palatable. To make one, you'll want to have:

- A permanent marker
- Herbs, spices, garlic, extracts, and bouillon cubes (See page 49 for more details.)
- A gallon-sized plastic zipper bag (If you can't find one, a sturdy plastic shopping bag is the next best thing.)
- A collection of tiny, snack-sized plastic zipper bags, or small plastic bags with twist-ties. (If your spices are coming from the bulk jars at the grocery store and are already in their own small bags, you don't need these.)

To make your spice bag, fill each of your small baggies with an herb or spice, labeling it with its proper name. Even if you know them all by sight or smell, a label is a good idea for when you're trying to find something in a hurry.

Now, seal the bags carefully and place them into the larger bag along with a head of garlic, container of bouillon cubes, and little vials of vanilla and almond extract. Voilà! Your spice bag is ready to roll.

# PACKING YOUR SPICE BAG

Below, I've compiled (in alphabetical order) a more specific breakdown of what to pack. Remember: you can carry more herbs and spices than the ones I've outlined, and you should collect new flavors as you travel!

## Basil

Basil marries well with tomatoes, and adds a delicious flavor to soups in conjunction with oregano and thyme. If your basil doesn't smell like anything, it's probably time to replace it.

## Bouillon cubes

Bouillon cubes are essential additions to camp cuisine, adding hearty, savory, meaty flavor to soups and stews. There's a wide variety of bouillon cubes out there, but I generally use chicken flavor, which is what the dishes in this book call for.

Buy expensive cubes or cheap ones, with or without MSG, depending on your preferences. If all you can find are bouillon *granules*, know that one cube (as called for in a recipe) is equal to one teaspoon of granules. The granules dissolve more quickly, but I prefer the cubes simply because they're easier to store.

## Cayenne pepper & chili flakes

Yowza! A tiny bit of cayenne pepper or a sprinkling of chili flakes can add considerable heat to a recipe. As a lover of spice, I don't travel anywhere without them. If you can't handle the heat though, there's no harm in leaving them out.

## Chili powder

Not to be confused with spicy chili flakes, this usually mild-flavored crimson spice blend is composed of chili peppers, cumin, oregano, garlic, and salt. I don't normally advocate carrying spice blends, as individual spices are often more versatile, but I make an exception for chili powder. It's delicious on fried potatoes, or as the star ingredient in chili con carne (page 164).

### Cinnamon
Though it's used in some parts of the world for savory cuisine, cinnamon is my favorite for sweets, pairing wonderfully with honey and sugar. It's delicious in crepes, oatmeal, granola, and other breakfast favorites.

### Cumin
Cumin adds a warm, vaguely smoky flavor to food. In this book, I use it mainly to season Tex-Mex-inspired dishes.

### Curry powder
This golden-colored staple is another spice blend that I don't mind carrying. It's good for making simple curries, sprinkling on hard-boiled eggs, or acting as the key flavoring in Berlin-style *currywurst* (page 205).

### Garlic (fresh)
The spice bag is a great place to store my favorite flavoring agent: fresh garlic. Always keep a head on hand for use in savory dishes of all kinds.

Good, fresh garlic cloves are firm when squeezed and should emit juice when you prick them with your fingernail. On the road, however, you don't always have the luxury of using the freshest ingredients—I've certainly cooked with my fair share of sad, shriveled garlic! There's nothing wrong with using garlic that has sprouted (the kind with a green shoot growing in the center of each clove) but it can have a bitter flavor. I use it anyway, but if it bothers you, pluck out the shoot.

## *Garlic granules*
Though fresh garlic is better for most things, I still love the flavor of garlic granules. If you can't find granules, use garlic powder. It's the same thing, really, just ground more finely.

## *Ginger (powdered)*
For Asian dishes such as stir-fries, be sure to have spicy powdered ginger on hand. Though less exciting than its fresh counterpart, it's a lot easier to carry and use.

## *Nutmeg & Cloves*
If you want to create the unmistakable aroma of autumn in your breakfasts or desserts, add nutmeg and cloves. They can also add rich depth of flavor to what would otherwise be ordinary tomato soup (page 176).

## *Onion powder*
I use fresh onions most of the time, but I find dried, powdered onion to be useful as well. If you're feeling lazy, or if you're in a sad, onion-less land, you can create a delicious meal seasoned with it.

## *Oregano*
Oregano is a wonderful addition to tomatoey Italian dishes, as well as any soups. I often like to combine it with basil and thyme. This herb is a star ingredient in my pot pie stew (page 178).

## *Paprika*
For a warm, earthy flavor in tomato-based sauces and soups, try paprika. I don't often call for it in this book's recipes, but I still recommend carrying a small amount with you. Better yet, try a spicy, smoked paprika!

### Pepper, black

Black pepper makes everything better. I always carry a disposable grinder full of whole peppercorns (in addition to a small bag of the pre-ground variety), so I can season my meals with freshly ground pepper.

### Rosemary

Spiky, needle-like rosemary leaves are crisp and fragrant, with what I find to be a slightly piney, minty flavor. I add the herb to soups, and use it as the star ingredient in such dishes as rosemary flatbread with garlic and chili flakes (page 226).

### Thyme

Bright, herby thyme is one of my favorite aromatics, though you wouldn't know it by looking through this book; the only recipe that calls for it specifically is pot pie stew (page 178). However, I frequently use thyme in soups when I invent them without a recipe (page 180).

### Vanilla extract & almond extract

In my opinion, vanilla and almond extracts are worth their weight in gold. Often sold in tiny, easy-to-pack bottles, they add precious flavor to breakfasts and sweet treats. Be sure to bring them along in your spice bag!

## SPICE ADVICE

- It's a fact of life that your spice bag won't stay perfectly organized indefinitely. Eventually, your pristine plastic zipper bag will become tattered and worn. Don't fret—it can be replaced with any sturdy sack.
- Purchase only very aromatic spices and herbs—if they don't smell like anything, they probably won't taste like anything, either! There are exceptions to this (hot chili flakes don't always have a smell, so be careful!), but it's a good rule of thumb.
- You don't always have to buy your spices at the supermarket. I picked wild sage (shown in the background photo) on a mountainside in Greece!
- Replace ziploc bags when their seals become so clogged with spice that they no longer close—you don't want to end up with spilled spices in all the nooks and crannies of your pannier!
- Should you find yourself with a spill or a build-up of various spices at the bottom of your bag, use it as a culinary experiment. Taste the spice blend and see what you think. Perhaps it's a candidate for sprinkling over fried eggs? Or maybe a pot of chili?

*Shopping in the morning market in Phou Khoun, Laos*

# SHOPPING AND PACKING

Whether you're topping up your supply of staple ingredients, or perusing the marketplace for your daily fix of fruits and vegetables, here are some shopping suggestions that should come in handy:

## *It's all about timing*
When you're shopping for meat and dairy, timing is important. If you're craving hamburgers for instance, keep a lookout for grocery stores towards the *end* of the cycling day. In this way, you can buy what you like, knowing you'll soon be at camp to cook it.

## *Sturdy matters*
It is very important to purchase bottles and cans that are capable of taking a beating. Look at all lids and caps for signs of weakness before you buy them. If possible, open and close them to judge their strength. If they're going to survive a jostling, bumpy life on the road, they'll need to be strong.

## *Think small*
Buy foods in the smallest quantities you can find, so you won't have to worry about how you'll fit them in your panniers, or how you'll use them before they go bad. Yes, buying small means you'll have to go shopping frequently, but that's just part of the process. You may even discover that you love the task—it's hard not to enjoy bantering with shopkeepers while discovering new foods and flavors!

### Add variety to your staples

Keep your eyes open for interesting, long-lasting foods that come in tiny, easily-packable containers—it's a great way to add variety to your stash of staples. I've come upon miniature cans of coconut milk, precious little jars of Thai curry paste, and a plethora of high-quality fish products in tiny tins, such as sardines and anchovies packed in flavored olive oil. What interesting items can you find in your part of the world?

### Think versatility

In the world of adventure travel, it is often thought of as foolhardy to have gear that serves only one purpose. A general rule of thumb is to make sure that everything you carry can perform at least two or three different tasks. In other words, the usability and versatility of every item is important.

This same concept applies in the mobile kitchen. For instance, a packet of pre-mixed "Italian" seasoning is unappealing to me because of its single purpose. Instead, I opt to carry a variety of individual spices that can be combined in innumerable ways. A jar of spaghetti sauce is less useful to me than a jar of tomato paste, which could become any number of things *besides* just spaghetti. Always keep the versatility of what you're purchasing in mind.

### Always buy the mystery can

When you visit a country whose language is utterly indecipherable to you, there will be food products available in the grocery store that are equally mysterious. My advice? Embrace the unknown! Buy that mystery can and give it a shot. The weirder the label, the more fun it is to taste. This is what travel is all about!

*This Macedonian mystery can turned out to be goulash!*

# FOOD FOR FREE

With our slow pace and connection to the landscape around us, we bicycle travelers are sometimes in the right place at the right time to find free food.

Rambling along little-used country roads means that we're in a fantastic position to harvest wild edibles... if we know where to look. Why not carry a pocket-sized plant identification book in your handlebar bag so you know what's safe to pick? On our journey, we made soups, stuffings, salads, and and sauces from an array of foraged foods: wild sage, garlic, blackberries, sorrel, and dandelion greens.

Cycling past farmers' fields just after harvest is nearly as exciting as foraging. In Italy, we followed the example of an elderly man and scoured the fields, gleaning armfuls of perfectly good tomatoes that had been overlooked by the harvester. We feasted for days on pasta and free, homemade tomato sauce!

Keep an eye on the roadsides, too, for farmers' castoffs. It made my day to pass a mountain of discarded eggplant and a heap of rapidly-wilting basil by the side of a country lane in Italy! Though the produce wasn't pretty enough to sell at the market, it was good enough for us. It's amazing what treasures you can find in someone else's compost heap!

Now, let's talk about what happens when you emerge from the discount supermarket with three giant shopping bags in tow, only to find yourself face to face with your dirty bicycle. What were you thinking? Those weather-worn panniers look awfully small compared to your grocery bags! But never fear—here's how to lighten your load and make everything fit.

### Re-Pot
You'll need to "re-pot" things (as Tyler likes to say), if you want to fit everything in your panniers. This means re-packing purchased items, removing their unwieldy packaging, and transferring them to containers that fit them better. You should also re-pot items that have weak paper packaging, like flour and sugar.

### Recycle
Unnecessary and difficult-to-pack cardboard boxes should be recycled if possible. Their contents, whether they be energy bars, a bag of cereal, or individually-wrapped cracker packets, will be much easier to fit in your panniers without bulky cardboard around them.

### Compress
When you find yourself with poofy, air-filled bags of cereal or crackers, prick a tiny hole in an inconspicuous corner, and then slowly press out the air. This will save a considerable amount of space in your panniers.

### Strap
Bungee nets are an indispensable part of any touring kit, allowing you to securely attach just about anything to the rack-pack of your bike. Shove any goodies that won't fit in your panniers under your bungee net until you can find space for them elsewhere.

# NOTES FROM OUR DAILY JOURNAL

"We carried on, exhausted but cheery at the prospect of stopping early and enjoying a huge, cold tub of ice cream. As we rolled into town we spotted a "Leader Price" discount grocer. Discount indeed! We found a package of three ice cream bars for €0.79 and promptly devoured them before returning to the store to restock our supplies. Feeling like kids in a candy shop, surrounded by cheap food and filled with a fierce hunger, we went… a little overboard.

We filled every single nook and cranny of our bicycles with food and then strapped the rest of it to the outside of our bikes! I felt a little sheepish about my insistence that we purchase a 2 lb. bag of carrots when it came time to find space for it on my fully-loaded rear rack. I was tempted to propose that we eat them all before leaving, but instead managed to squeeze them under a couple of bungee cords. Laughing at ourselves, we teetered precariously out of the parking lot down to camp…"

## *Wrap*

To prevent leaks and spills, double-wrap bottles of liquid (including your fuel bottle) in plastic bags. As well, do your best to store them upright. Trust me, it's no fun to find the soy sauce you just purchased pooling at the bottom of your pannier.

## *Foiled again*

Carrying a small roll of tinfoil is a good idea, as is tucking away some zip-top plastic bags. They're not the most environmentally friendly forms of packaging, but having these tools on hand sure does make storing food a lot easier. Store tinfoil vertically in the back pocket of your cooking pannier.

After you've managed to cram everything into or onto your bike and you've teetered your way to the nearest campsite or farmer's field, it's time to re-organize all that food into a nicely managed system.

There are three things a good pannier organization system should allow you to do. First, your setup should allow you to find snacks easily. Second, it should make it easy to keep tabs on fresh goods so they don't rot. And third, it should make it easy for you to quickly grab what you need to start dinner.

Here, I've outlined some tips to create a storage system that will help you achieve all of those objectives. It is an especially good solution for those travelling in pairs (who can share the load), who also carry Ortlieb panniers (which don't have much in the way of pockets or compartments). There are no hard and fast rules here, however. As always, do what works for you.

### The snack pannier
Within the walls of my snack pannier (a small pannier at the front of my bike) reside all manner of tasty, ready-to-eat foods that are practical to munch on at any time. Carrots, cookies, crackers, cured meats, cheeses, leftovers, and fruits... this is all fair game. I also keep a small jar of salt in here, in case I want to sprinkle it over vegetables or leftovers.

Keeping pantry items separate from your snacks means that you'll never have to sift through them hungrily in search of something to eat. The last thing you want to do at the top of a difficult mountain climb is tear apart your panniers looking for food!

### The pantry pannier
In this small pannier, I keep the everyday food items that need some preparing. Everything from fresh potatoes and onions to canned beans and tomatoes get stored in here. Plastic canisters of flour and sugar, plus a container of cooking salt, make their homes in here as well. The wide, flat pocket at the back of Ortlieb panniers is a great place for storing packages of noodles.

### The cooking pannier
Chock full of all the tools I need to make dinner, this large pannier is the first thing I reach for when it's time to cook. My cookset takes up much of the room in here; inside of it live my small collapsible mugs and bowls, a camp stove, lighter, can opener, and vegetable peeler. The metal items are stored in a cloth sack, so they don't scratch the cookset's non-stick surface.

Around the cookset, I pack a bottle of dishwashing soap (standing upright so as to prevent spills), a spice bag, and a large bottle of olive oil (also standing upright to prevent spills). A rag for drying dishes is stuffed in there somewhere as well.

In the wide, flat pocket at the back of the pannier, I store wooden cooking utensils, a folded-up wind screen, a scrub brush for dishwashing, a gigantic bowie knife (in its sturdy sheath), a large cutting board, and a large collapsible plate.

## *Miscellaneous items to be stored*

What about the many things that don't seem to fit in the snack, pantry, or cooking panniers? I store my fuel bottle (wrapped in a plastic bag) at the top of any pannier that doesn't have food in it.

Meanwhile, often-used items, like sporks, lighters, and pocket knives, are kept in my handlebar bag for easy access. My handlebar bag is generally also home to an energy bar or two, in case I need to have a post-cycling, pre-cooking snack.

> ❗ *Weight distribution matters! Make sure opposing panniers are approximately the same heft or your bicycle will be unwieldy, and difficult to steer.*

📷 We spotted this butterfly on one of our panniers in Thailand

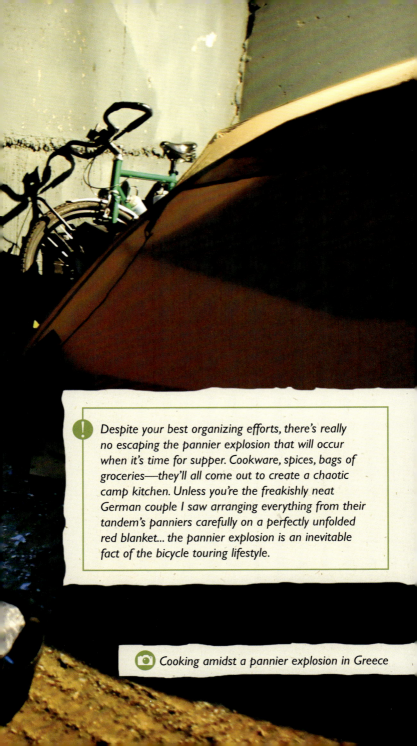

> ❗ Despite your best organizing efforts, there's really no escaping the pannier explosion that will occur when it's time for supper. Cookware, spices, bags of groceries—they'll all come out to create a chaotic camp kitchen. Unless you're the freakishly neat German couple I saw arranging everything from their tandem's panniers carefully on a perfectly unfolded red blanket... the pannier explosion is an inevitable fact of the bicycle touring lifestyle.

📷 *Cooking amidst a pannier explosion in Greece*

# IN THE CAMP KITCHEN

*Cooking on the banks of the Danube River in Romania*

# CAMP COOKING BASICS

Now that your groceries are purchased and your pedal-powered pantry is ready for action, it's time to familiarize yourself with the camp kitchen. In this section, we'll discuss the basic tenets of cooking on the road, and introduce some troubleshooting ideas that will help you avoid common pitfalls.

## *Use non-stick cookware, and take care of it*

I've said it before and I'll say it again: to successfully prepare many of the recipes in this book, **you need to use non-stick cookware.** I've had horrible luck cooking in stainless steel pans on the road, and even worse luck trying to clean the resulting burnt-on messes. (Think overnight soaks and laborious scrubbing sessions.) For the sake of your sanity when cooking and dishwashing off the beaten path, get non-stick cookware.

To ensure that your non-stick pans last as long as possible without their surfaces scratching and chipping, use wooden or silicone utensils instead of metal, and make sure that anything stored in your cookset is well-wrapped. As well, never leave an empty pan on the stove while you're cooking.

## *Avoid cooking while* **hangry**

Have you ever been so hungry that you lost your ability to think and act rationally? So hungry that you became enraged at the slightest inconvenience, illogically and hysterically upset like a tearful two-year-old? Yep, me too. That's what I call being HANGRY. Needless to say, it's best not to attempt cooking while you're hangry unless you're a fan of charred, angst-filled food. If you're ready to have a tantrum after the day's ride, eat a snack, put on some comfy pants, and relax for a bit before you start. Then, if you feel up to it, begin preparing your food. Sometimes, I find chopping vegetables into tiny pieces oddly calming when my brain is fried.

### Keep it simple at first

For the best outcome, don't try recipes that are labeled "expert" unless you're in the mood for a messy and delicious project. Additionally, don't attempt them for the first time when you're exhausted or famished. Instead, wait until you have plenty of time, water, patience, and enthusiasm at the ready. The same goes for any recipes with techniques you're not familiar with. Keep it simple and easy at first, then build up to the harder stuff.

### Assess your water supply

Always assess your water supply before you begin cooking so as not to find yourself lacking. Are you at a campsite where you have plenty of hot water to use for soups, stews, and washing dishes? Are you free camping near a clean stream that you could use for rinsing plates and bowls? If you cook a brothy soup, will your remaining water supply last until you can re-fill on the road tomorrow morning?

### Get to know your cook stove

Though I provide tips for using your stove on the next page and offer instructions for dealing with these fire-breathing beasts in each individual recipe, I can't actually show you in person how to use yours. If this is your first outing, practice priming and lighting your stove *before* you attempt the recipes in this book.

# COOKIN' WITH GAS

When you use a Whisperlight stove as I do, it can be tricky getting used to its idiosyncrasies. Let's talk about a few concepts that will help get you cooking:

The Whisperlite must be pre-heated or "primed" in order to make it hot enough to vaporize its liquid fuel. Some people carry alcohol for this purpose because it burns cleanly, but we like to keep things simple. In this photo, we're priming our stove with sooty, unleaded gasoline right from the fuel bottle. After the priming flame goes out, the fuel line will be hot enough to vaporize the gas and produce a powerful blue flame.

When you want to cook multiple dishes in a row, try re-lighting your stove without priming it each time. As long as the fuel line is still hot, you should be able to light it without pre-heating it again.

When you want to use very low heat, try unscrewing your fuel bottle to de-pressurize it. Screw it back on, then pressurize it slightly by giving it just two or three pumps before you light it. This will produce a low heat flame. You may have to pump it a few times while cooking to keep the pressure up.

## *Read the directions, even if you don't follow them*

Read the recipe before you begin cooking. No really, read the *entire* recipe before you begin. Read it several times even, so you get a feel for what to expect. I do my best to guide you, but I don't want you to be surprised and flustered at any point during the process.

## *Be prepared*

I'll talk more about this in the next section, but I'll say it here first because it's important: **prepare your ingredients first and have them ready before you light your stove.** A hot blue flame brings excitement, drama and elevated nerves to your camp kitchen—don't add to the chaos by scrambling around trying to prepare things as you go.

## *Check your gas*

Give your fuel bottle a quick shake before you begin cooking so you know approximately how much gasoline remains. This will save you from the disappointing scenario in which you begin to fry up a big pan of potatoes, only to have your flame peter out and die, leaving you with an unappetizing meal of crunchy, greasy, half-cooked spuds. Trust me, it isn't fun!

## *Keep a hand on the pan*

The cooking process happens quickly! Take your eyes off a frying egg for a second, and you'll find yourself with a rubbery, overcooked mess. So that this bummer of an example doesn't happen to you, *always keep a hand on your frying pan* so you're ready at a moment's notice to move it around, lift it above the flame, or remove it from the heat altogether. (Just make sure it's balanced when you set it back on the stove, or your meal might spill onto the ground!)

I sometimes make exceptions to the hand-on-the pan rule, namely when I'm simmering soup, or boiling pasta and potatoes. In those cases, there's usually plenty of liquid to prevent scorching, and the food cooks at a much more relaxed pace.

### Cool it off

A corollary to the keep-a-hand-on-the-pan rule is the cool-it-off rule. If you're freaking out about how hot your stove is and how fast your food is cooking (or burning, heaven forbid!), *take the pan off the flame.* It's really okay to simply set it in the grass while you regroup, take a deep breath, and assess the problem.

If the stressful situation isn't quite that dire but you still want to slow cooking down a bit, raise the pan a couple of inches above the stove. I often hold the pan above the stove, regardless of what I'm making.

# PREPARING YOUR INGREDIENTS

One of the best ways to minimize stress in the camp kitchen is to prepare everything you'll need to make a recipe before you ever light your stove. This means emptying your cooking pannier, assembling your cook stove, getting out your knives and cutting boards, and preparing your ingredients. You'll also measure spices, open cans, and chop vegetables. Onions and potatoes will be cubed for soup, or garlic minced for a pasta dish, or green beans cleaned and snapped in half for a stir-fry.

I go into specific detail about how to prepare your ingredients in each recipe, but here is a bit of general guidance to help you get a few basics ready (in alphabetical order).

### *Avocados (how to cut them)*

Those green, leathery, prehistoric-looking fruits are actually not as intimidating as they might first appear. An avocado is ripe when the little nub of its stem pushes easily into the fruit, or when it no longer feels hard as a rock when squeezed—it should have the tiniest bit of give, but it shouldn't feel mushy.

To use an avocado, slice it vertically, cutting all the way around the large central pit. Separate the halves by twisting them apart. Next, remove the pit by karate-chopping it with your knife, and twisting to dislodge it. Then, you can cut the flesh into slices or checkerboard patterns, being careful not to break the skin. Finally, scrape out the flesh, and it's ready for use in a recipe.

### *Broccoli (how to chop it)*

There is only one broccoli recipe in this book, but if you like it as much as I do, you'll be making it often. In case you're unsure how to prepare broccoli for cooking, here we go: chop about a half-inch off the end of the broccoli's stem and discard it. If the skin of the stem is very thick, you can peel it off (but you don't *have* to). Next, chop the stem into pieces, and cut the florets (the flowery bits at the top) into approximately equal-sized chunks. Now, you're ready to stir-fry them, steam them, plop them into a soup, or prepare them any way you like.

### *Cabbage (how to chop it)*

For the lone cabbage recipe in this book, choose the smallest one you can find at the market. Hack off the tough end, and then cut the vegetable in half. Lay it flat-side down on your cutting board, and cut it in half again. Now, with a quarter of the vegetable, slice thinly so you end up with squiggly ribbons. Cut as much as you need in this way, and then wrap the rest in a plastic bag to use tomorrow.

### *Cheese (how to measure it)*

To get a rough estimate, you can think of one ounce of cheese being the size of four dice stacked on top of one another. If you're really having trouble with this, just remember an easy rule: more cheese is always better.

### *Garlic (how to mince it)*

First, separate a clove from your head of garlic and remove the peel. Smashing it first with the flat side of a knife will make this easier. After that, cut the clove into tiny little bits. That's all there is to it—it sounds simple because it is!

If I don't have a cutting surface handy, I'll sometimes hold a peeled clove between my thumb and forefinger, cutting thin slices into it, stopping just before I reach the end. Then, I'll rotate the clove ninety degrees, and do the same thing again, making a checkerboard pattern. Finally, I slice it crosswise so that as tiny, precut pieces of garlic fall off the end and into the pan. This is not the most efficient method in the world, but it will save you from having to clean a cutting board. On the other hand, you'll probably wind up with little bits of garlic stuck to your fingers. There's no escaping cleaning something!

### *Jalapeño (how to cut it)*
Slice the stem end off the jalapeño and then cut the pepper in half lengthwise. Scrape out the seeds (or leave them in if you like the heat), then cut the pepper into thin, matchstick-sized slices. Cut those crosswise until you're left with tiny pieces.

Be careful where you put your hands after you're through slicing jalapenos—don't pick your nose or wipe your eyes without thoroughly washing your hands first. Otherwise, you'll be in for a painful surprise!

### *Leeks (how to clean them)*
Leeks are deceptively dirty. To prepare, slice them open lengthwise and fan them out. You will most likely find some dirt and sand between the layers. If you do, rinse them off in a basin of water, or squirt them with your water bottle until clean. Once free of dirt, the leeks can be sliced (flat side on your cutting board) into half-moon shapes, or prepared as called for in a recipe.

### Lemons & Limes (how to juice them)
The best way I've found to juice lemons or limes without access to a nice wooden citrus reamer is to first roll the fruits on any hard surface. This will loosen up the juices. Next, slice the fruit in half crosswise. Then, stick a metal spork or knife into the flesh with one hand, while twisting and squeezing the fruit with the other. Be careful not to pierce the citrus rind and stab the palm of your hand!

### Mango (how to cut it)
A mango is a strange fruit, so if you've never tried one, it can be a little daunting to approach. But don't worry, you can do it, especially with the help of the step-by-step photo tutorial on page 141.

### Onions (how to chop and mince them)
The name of the game here is to get the onion into roughly equal-sized, smallish chunks. To do this, cut the onion vertically from its root to its tip. Lay each half flat-side down on your cutting board, and slice off the ends. Remove and discard the peel, and then cut one of your onion halves into a checkerboard pattern, first in vertical strips, and then in perpendicular strips. If it is a large onion, you may have to cut some of the resulting pieces in half. Do the same with the second half of the onion, or wrap it in a bag to save for later.

### Potatoes (how to prepare them)
Honestly, I never bother peeling potatoes. You may feel differently about the matter, and that's fine—you'll just have to bring a vegetable peeler with you, or get good at peeling with your pocket knife. If you're a non-peeler like me, rinse the potatoes, or at the very least, make sure the outsides are relatively clean. Cut off any bad

spots, and remove any "eyes" where the potato is beginning to sprout.

From here, how you cut a potato depends on what you're cooking. When I instruct you to "cube" a potato, I mean you should cut the potato into cube-like chunks with sides roughly a centimeter wide (a little bigger than a quarter of an inch). Do this on a cutting board, or, try the hand-held technique I mentioned in the garlic section (page 79).

When I cook fried potatoes, I slice them into thin rounds, though that choice is purely arbitrary. Don't obsess about this stuff. Just know that the smaller you cut the potato, the faster it will cook.

## *Tomatoes (how to chop them)*

In most recipes, you're going to want chunks of tomatoes. So, remove the stem, and, with the serrated part of your pocket knife, cut the tomato in half from the stem-end to the bottom. If you don't have a serrated portion on your pocket knife, or if your smooth edge is dull, pierce the tomato's skin first, and then start slicing at that spot. Place one half of the tomato flat-side up on your cutting board. Now cut it into crescents if you wish, or keep slicing if you're aiming for chunks.

## *Zucchini (how to prepare them)*

Choose a small, skinny zucchini, and cut off the stem. Next, slice the zucchini in half lenghwise. Rest the halves on your cutting board, flat-side down, and cut them into strips. Slice the strips crosswise to get small chunks. For zucchini feta fritters (page 214) you'll want *very* small pieces so they'll hold together in batter—keep halving the chunks until they're the size of corn kernels.

Tyler cutting onions and cheese in Macedonia

> Vegetables cook fastest when the pieces are small and of a uniform thickness. That's all you really need to know. Don't stress about the rest—this is not an episode of Top Chef; this is your supper, and you're in the wilderness. It is supposed to be rustic. Just chop it to bits and you'll be fine!

# EVERYTHING BUT THE KITCHEN SINK

Without a sink in your camp kitchen to provide a ready supply of hot and cold water, how can you fill pasta pots, rinse veggies, or wash the dishes? It's time to tackle those questions and more in this section about water.

## How much water?

In addition to the drinking water you carry to keep you hydrated throughout the day, as a cycling cook you're going to need an extra supply. If you're not staying at hotels or campsites where you have reliable access to this precious resource, I recommend carrying one to three litres with you, *in addition to drinking water*, for your daily cooking and dishwashing needs. Carry this liquid in whatever containers suit you: water bottles of metal or BPA-free plastic, hydration bladders, or re-purposed soda bottles. Our favorite is a sturdy orange soda bottle that we bungee to the rack-pack of Tyler's bike.

The variability in the amount of water you should bring is dependent upon what you intend to cook. If you're planning to boil pasta or make soup, you'll need plenty of water to fill your large pot, plus more for dishwashing. Thus, you should carry on the three-litre end of the spectrum. If you'd like to prepare a salad on the other hand, you'll just need a bit of water with which to rinse veggies and clean vinaigrette from your dishes. Thus, you can carry on the one-litre side.

If, like me, you're scared of unexpectedly entering a freak desert-like region and dying a slow death of dehydration, always have an ample, 3-litre supply on hand.

## *Where can I fill up?*

It's a good idea to fill your water bottles when the opportunity arises instead of waiting until you're down to your last drop. Here are some ideas of places where you can replenish your supply:

- Water spigots are usually found next to the air spigots at gas stations. Gas station bathrooms also usually have faucets.

- Potable water fountains can be found in many towns across Europe. We had especially good luck finding fountains in Switzerland and Romania.

*Filling our repurposed soda bottle at a Romanian fountain*

- Restaurant staff are usually happy to refill your bottles with water (and ice, if you're lucky), especially if you've spent money at their establishment.

- Gas station attendants and fast food chain workers across the USA are never bothered when Tyler and I fill our bottles with ice water at the self-serve drink station.

- Check near cemeteries—there's nearly always a spigot or fountain of some kind so mourners can water the flowers they bring.

- Ask someone friendly-looking, who's outside mowing their lawn or gardening, if they'd be willing to fill your water bottles for you. If you're in a bind and there's no one to ask, try for spigots on the outsides of houses and garages where people might attach their gardening hoses.

## *Washing the dishes*

If you're anything like me, washing dishes on the road without the luxury of hot, running water can take some getting used to. It can be a harsh realization to find out that the standards of cleanliness we live by at home are simply not attainable on the road. In this section, I'll try to ease this transition by sharing my three favorite dishwashing techniques.

Let's begin with the fancy method, good for germophobes and newbie cycle tourists whose standards of cleanliness haven't yet been beaten out of them by the grime of the open road. First, get your large pot as clean as possible if it isn't already. (See how this could be a vicious cycle?) Fill it with water, and heat it over your stove until it's a comfortable temperature. Bear in mind that if it's chilly outside, it will cool down quickly—better to have overly hot water than a rapidly cooling supply. This is going to be both your washing water and your rinsing water, so don't add soap to it.

Take your cleanest dish and squirt a bit of eco-friendly dish soap on it (if you can find some). Pour in a bit of hot water, and, using a long handled scrubber, wash it. When you're done with that one, pour the still-hot, relatively clean water into the next cleanest dish. Keep washing in order of cleanest to dirtiest, discarding water when it becomes disgusting, and adding fresh hot water and soap when you need it. Rinse dishes by pouring in a little bit of hot water, sloshing it around, and pouring it into the next dish. Continue until all the dishes are clean. Let the them air-dry (unless it's cold out, in which case, wipe them off before the water freezes onto them), and stow them neatly away in your panniers.

The second dishwashing method (possible only with non-stick cookware) is by far my favorite. It's easy, practical, and aligned with the reality that the bicycle touring lifestyle is anything but hygienic and perfect—*If you can't see any gunk on the pot, it's clean... right?*

First, use a piece of bread to wipe up any remaining soup or sauce from your pans and dishes. Then, eat the bread. Finish the job with a swipe from a small, wet towel. Tyler and I carry a small rag with us for just this purpose, discarding it and buying a new one when it gets too gross for comfort.

My third and final dishwashing technique? If you're traveling in a couple or group, see if you can get someone *else* to do the dishes. After all, you did the cooking!

# WINGING IT

Being able to improvise is an indispensable skill on a bike tour, and it comes in handy in the kitchen as well. It is my hope that after making the recipes in this book once or twice, you will gain the confidence and skill needed to strike out on your own into deliciously uncharted recipe-less lands. In this section, I provide some final food for thought that should come in especially handy when you're trying to wing it.

## Use your senses

Using your senses (especially smell, touch, and taste) will help you become a more skilled, intuitive cook.

***Smell:*** Smell your spices! They should be fragrant. Hold them close to the dish you're considering seasoning, and sniff so you can get a sense of how they would go together. Do the two marry well, or do they clash?

***Sight & Touch:*** After you measure your herb or spice according to the recipe, dump it into the palm of your hand so you can get a feel for it. How big of a mound does a tablespoon make? What about a teaspoon? Could you estimate that amount if you had to?

***Taste:*** To really be the arbiter of your own culinary destiny, you need to taste the food you're cooking as you go. The time to taste a dish isn't at the end, when you're surprised by the flavors, but at each point along the way. You're the one that's going to be eating the food, and you know what you like better than any cookbook author or recipe writer ever will. So, be sure to taste between each addition, and always trust your instincts over a recipe.

📷 *"Winging it" at suppertime in buggy Siberia*

❗ *Your cooking experiments might not turn out exactly as you hope the first time, but the more you try new things, the more you'll learn, adding valuable skills to your culinary repertoire.*

## Get creative & be resourceful

Culinary independence comes when you use your creative ingenuity. Have you ever had to repair your tent poles using only the random materials you had on hand? Have you ever had to fix a cracked rim with duct tape so you could limp ten miles to the next town? It's time to extend the same McGuyver-esque creativity to your cycling kitchen.

While you're riding, think about the foods you have on hand, and brainstorm about the different ways you could use them to create a satisfying meal. Could you cook a yummy supper without spending money at the grocery store? Could you do it without letting anything to go to waste? Get your culinary imagination flowing, just as you would for any other challenge you face.

> Don't have a grater, but you'd really like one? Make one out of a tin can, punching holes in the side of it with your knife point. Don't have a double boiler, but want to experiment with a recipe that requires one? Fill your cooking pot with water, and set your frying pan on top. Use your ingenuity to create what you need!

## *Cook fresh*

It's easy to cook well without a recipe when you're working with the freshest of locally grown, in-season foods. A new spring radish needs little but a sprinkling of salt and a slice of thickly buttered baguette to render it a masterpiece. A single juicy plum needs no adornment. A crimson tomato, fat and sun-ripened, needs nothing but a touch of sea salt.

Fry up some of summer's finest green beans with minced garlic in a small pool of olive oil. Toss in some cooked pasta, and you'll create a fine supper. Most in-season vegetables need little preparation, and it's hard to mess them up.

## *Substitute*

Depending on where you are in the world and what season it is, chances are you'll occasionally have to substitute for some ingredients called for in the recipes.

For instance, if you can't find potatoes where you are, try cooking with sweet potatoes, white sweet potatoes, rutabagas, or turnips. Instead of using broccoli in a stir-fry, try green beans, Chinese kale, or even eggplant. The recipe might not turn out exactly as intended when you substitute ingredients, but that's okay—this is an adventure!

## *Flavor, flavor, flavor*

Say you're improvising a meal, but it's just kind of dull and uninspiring? Perhaps you just need more seasoning! The tips on the following page will help you troubleshoot your meals when something seems off.

# SEASONING SECRETS

### Add salt
If your food is bland, perhaps a bit of salt would help. A small amount won't make the dish taste salty, but it will bring out the flavor of the food itself.

### Add acidity
If salt didn't help the blandness, try adding a squeeze of lemon juice or a drop of vinegar to brighten things up.

### Add sweetness
Too much acidity can be balanced with sweetness. Add some sugar (just a dash at a time), or even a touch of honey. You don't want the food to taste overly sweet; you only want to add enough to balance the flavors.

### Add savoriness
Add more herbs! Add more spices! Refer to the spice bag section (page 47) to see which herbs and spices go well together. Try adding a bouillon cube or two for some meaty, salty, savoriness.

### Add fat
Even a small dab of butter can create more depth of flavor in your meal. I've found that a touch of fat helps meld disparate flavors together in delicious harmony.

### Add alcohol
If you happen to have some, a splash of white wine in a creamy pasta dish is heaven, while a bit of rum makes a nice addition to warm, buttery fruity desserts.

> By winging it, you can create some deliciously memorable meals. This impromptu supper of Indian-spiced eggplant with Romanian smashed beans, a fried egg, and a homemade tortilla (see page 222) remains, to this day, the tastiest creation I've ever made on the road!

*Garlic chives in a market in Kampong Chhnang, Cambodia*

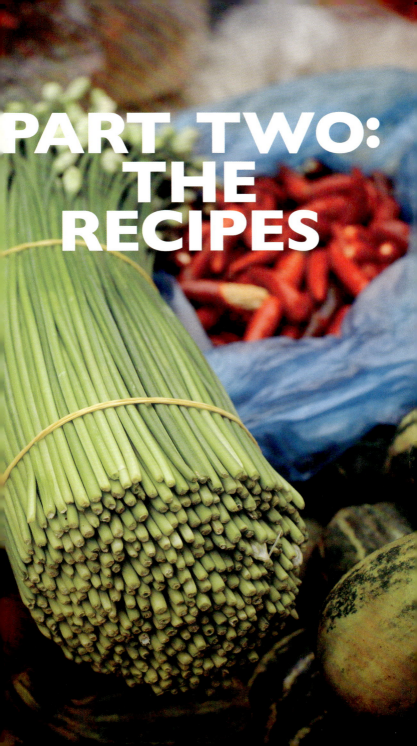

# PART TWO: THE RECIPES

# NOTES ON THE RECIPES

## *On the layout & instructions*

The recipe instructions in this book are tailored for use with an MSR Whisperlite camp stove. You can certainly use something else, but you may have to be liberal in your interpretation of temperatures for successful results. For example, when I use the term "low heat", it should be read loosely as "whatever temperature you have that isn't going to scorch your food," while "high heat" can be thought of as "whatever temperature is going to boil water the fastest."

    Each recipe is labeled with the approximate time it takes to make, and how many people it serves. Keep in mind that you might be a slow cook at first. You might also be hungrier than I've anticipated, so serving sizes could be a little off. Eventually, though, you and I will get the hang of cooking together.

    Each recipe is also labeled with a difficulty rating. "**Easy**" recipes are fairly straightforward, usually involving one pot, and few ingredients. Start with these if you're new at cooking on the road. "**Moderate**" means you should pay attention, as there may be multiple steps or tricky parts. "**Expert**" means you should read the recipe several times, follow it carefully, and be aware of long cooking times, multiple steps, or complicated actions. Only attempt them when you're in a good mood, not too famished, and have the energy for a fun project. If you don't get the recipe right the first time, don't worry—just try again when you feel up to it.

    The recipes in this book use a unique measuring system specifically tailored for the mobile cook: everything is calculated in teaspoons and tablespoons. Even quantities that would normally be written in cups are intentionally written in the equivalent of tablespoons, so you don't need to worry about carrying a cup measure along with you. I do provide cup measurements as well, however, in case you find that easier.

## On the ingredients:

You'll find loads of garlic, chili flakes, and butter within these pages, because I have a deep fondness for all three.

You won't find too many recipes involving meat in this book, and the reason for that is simple: I don't eat it very often when I'm touring. An exception to this is cured meat, which I enjoy having on hand, as it keeps for a couple of days, and adds wonderful flavor to foods.

When I call for butter in a recipe, I mean salted butter. Use what you can find in your area, however, and adjust salt levels accordingly.

If you're a vegetarian, feel free to omit the occasional usage of meat in this book. Instead, bulk up your dishes with slices of thick, beefy mushrooms, or an extra can of beans, or experiment with adding a quick-cooking grain like quinoa. Use vegetable bouillon cubes instead of chicken.

If you're vegan, you can use olive oil instead of butter in most of the recipes, and vegetable bouillon instead of chicken. Leave out the cheese, and feel free to substitute a bit of sugar or maple syrup for the occasional usage of honey. I haven't tested the recipes to be vegan-friendly, however.

It is my aim to provide recipes and ideas that are geared towards using the same set of basic, long-lasting, staple ingredients. Thus, many of my recipes rely on *cans* of things. I did this intentionally, so that when you're faced with a minimarket stuffed full of them, or when you must travel for several days without resupplying, you'll still be able to cook something delicious. *However*, if you do have access to fresh vegetables and fresh dairy, please, for the love of all things holy, use them. Everything will taste better when you do.

Finally, the recipes in this book are heavily spiced for a reason. Since we're aiming to cook quickly, without long periods of simmering on the stove to develop flavors, the seasonings need to be strong and present from the get-go.

Now, with all of that in mind, get out there and start cooking, my friends!

> But wait! Do you have your non-stick pot and pan at the ready? You need non-stick cookware to make the recipes in this book—otherwise, you may be left with a burned-on mess. Consider yourself warned!

Light streaming through the trees in Germany

# BREAKFAST
## (AND SECOND BREAKFAST)

*This crunchy, caramelized, camp-friendly granola is extremely tasty, and far more exciting than its humble list of ingredients would seem to indicate. For more substance, add four tablespoons of nuts along with the oats and raisins. If you want to make more granola than the recipe calls for, make it in separate batches.*

# cinnamon raisin granola

*Prep & cook time: 10 minutes*
*Makes: 1 cup of granola*
*Difficulty: easy*

2 tablespoons butter
2 tablespoons sugar
1 teaspoon cinnamon
a pinch of salt
12 tablespoons (¾ cup) rolled oats
4 tablespoons (¼ cup) raisins

First, get your ingredients ready: measure the butter, sugar, cinnamon, and salt into your large cooking pot. Measure the oats and raisins into a bowl and set aside. Now, get cooking: prime and light your stove, turning it to a low setting. Holding your pot an inch or two above the flame, stir the mixture together for a minute, or until it is completely melted and very bubbly. Dump in the oats and raisins, and stir continuously for about two minutes, or until the oats smell very toasted. Remove the pan from the heat—the granola will still look a bit damp at this point, but it will crispen as it cools.

Once cool, enjoy the granola with or without milk, or store it in a container to snack on later.

## EGG ADVICE:

- When purchasing, seek out large, fresh eggs from farmers who let their chickens roam free outdoors. They'll taste amazing and be good for you, too.
- If you can't find a hard surface on which to crack an egg, thwack it with the sharp edge of your pocket knife to create a clean break.
- Add eggs to your frying pan carefully and in the center, so as not to knock the pan off-balance. (Many lightweight camp frying pans are prone to flipping off the stove if you don't keep a hand on them when you add things—I've lost many a meal by accidentally knocking the pan into the grass!)
- Low and slow is the way to go when you're cooking eggs. If you can't coax your cook stove to a low setting, hold the pan above the flame.
- Much of the world doesn't use egg cartons. This can pose a problem for cyclists who need to keep their eggs intact while riding on bumpy roads! To remedy this situation, I hoard cartons when I find them and fortify them with duct tape. In this way, I can reuse them for a very long time.

A truck carrying eggs on a ferry to Kerkennah Island, Tunisia

*Whether you call it a toad-in-the-hole, egg-in-a-basket, or one-eyed-sailor, this dish couldn't be simpler or more suited to the camp kitchen. It's quick and easy to prepare, and there are only three main ingredients! Since you probably have them on hand already, there's no reason not to make a homemade breakfast before a riding day. The instructions below make a single one-eyed sailor, but you can double, triple, or quadruple the recipe depending on your hunger level.*

# one-eyed-sailor

*Prep & cook time: 10 minutes*
*Makes: 1 one-eyed-sailor*
*Difficulty: moderate*

1 slice bread
½ tablespoon butter
1 egg
Salt and pepper

First, get your ingredients ready: with your knife, cut a circle from the center of the bread. Then, add a pat of butter (about a half-tablespoon) to your frying pan. Get the egg out, and set it within reach.

Now, get cooking: prime and light your stove, turning it to a low setting. Melt the butter slowly, swirling the pan an inch or two above the heat if needed (you don't want the butter to bubble or brown). When the butter has melted, take the pan off the stove and set it in the grass. Add the slice of bread and crack the egg into the hole. Set the cut-out piece of bread in the pan, too. Holding the pan above the flame slightly, cook the one-eyed-sailor for a minute or two, checking the underside with your spatula for doneness. When it's a deep golden brown color, flip it over and cook the second side until it, too, is golden. Don't forget to keep tabs on the bread "hole," flipping it as necessary. Season with salt and pepper to taste.

*Start your day with cheesy, spicy scrambled eggs wrapped in a tortilla blanket. Use store-bought tortillas, or try your hand at making your own (see page 222). If you're really strapped for ingredients, you can simply skip the wrap altogether and enjoy the eggs on their own. The eggs are well-seasoned so you won't need any salsa, but a few avocado slices would be a nice accompaniment if you happen to have any.*

# spicy scrambled egg breakfast burrito

*Prep & cook time: 15 minutes*
*Makes: 1 burrito*
*Difficulty: easy*

2 eggs
½ teaspoon garlic granules
a generous pinch of cumin (I use ¼ teaspoon)
a generous sprinkling of chili flakes (I use ½ teaspoon)
a generous sprinkling of salt and pepper
1 teaspoon water
1 teaspoon oil
1 ounce (28 grams) Cheddar or Pepperjack cheese
a very small wedge of onion (1 tablespoon, minced)
1 large flour tortilla
avocado slices (optional)

First, prepare your ingredients: crack the eggs into your frying pan along with the garlic granules, cumin, chili flakes, salt, pepper, water, and oil. Slice the cheese finely, and mix it in as well. Mince the wedge of onion, and add it into the egg mixture. Get out your tortilla and set it aside.

Now, get cooking: prime and light your stove, turning it to a low setting. Holding the frying pan an inch or two above the flame, stir constantly, scraping the bottom of the pot with your wooden spoon. Continue until the eggs are scrambled and cooked, approximately one minute. Don't overdo it here—you want pillowy soft eggs, not dry crusty ones. Spoon the eggs into a tortilla, wrap them up, and enjoy.

A chicken taking shelter from the rain with us in Italy

*In this spiced-up version of classic fried eggs, the eggs are cooked in a delicious combination of garlic, chili, and herbs. Though I like my yolks runny, feel free to cook yours until they're as done as you please.*

# garlic-chili-herb fried eggs

*Prep & cook time: 15 minutes*
*Makes: 2 fried eggs*
*Difficulty: easy*

2 teaspoons olive oil
¼ teaspoon garlic granules
¼ teaspoon chili flakes
¼ teaspoon rosemary leaves, slightly broken
¼ teaspoon oregano
¼ teaspoon black pepper
salt to taste
2 eggs
a slice of buttered bread (optional)

Measure the olive oil and all of the herbs and spices into your frying pan, crushing the rosemary spikes slightly with your fingertips. Stir to combine. Crack the eggs into the pan, and season them liberally with salt.

Now, get cooking: prime and light your stove, turning it to a low setting. Holding the pan a couple inches above the flame, cook the eggs for about a minute until the bottoms are cooked and they look sturdy enough to flip. Separate the eggs, and flip them one by one. Fry until the white is cooked and the yolk is still soft. Serve over buttered bread, or eat as-is.

*On mornings when you're craving something a little more festive than your average bowl of porridge, go for this delicious alternative. The banana dissolves somewhat into the oatmeal, creating a creamy texture dotted with soft chunks. Don't skip the cinnamon, vanilla, peanut butter, or honey—they all add delightful depth of flavor.*

# banana nut oatmeal

*Prep & cook time: 10 minutes*
*Makes: 2 generous servings*
*Difficulty: easy*

1 ripe banana
16 tablespoons (1 cup) rolled oats
1 tablespoon sugar
32 tablespoons (2 cups, or 500 ml) water
a hefty pinch of salt
½ teaspoon cinnamon
½ teaspoon vanilla
2 tablespoons peanut butter
honey for drizzling

Cut the banana into slices or small chunks and add them to your large cooking pot. Then add the oats, sugar, water, and salt.

Now, get cooking: prime and light your stove, turning it to a low setting. Cook the oats, stirring constantly with your wooden spoon. When the oats are soft and the liquid has been absorbed, about three minutes, take the pot off the heat and add the cinnamon, vanilla, and peanut butter. Stir to combine, then drizzle each serving with honey.

*French toast is one of those wonderfully frugal foods you can make even if you're down to the dregs in your panniers. White bread, potato bread, or challah will produce a lovely custardy toast, while whole wheat will make a very hardy, substantial final product. If you use milk instead of water, you'll get even tastier results. Don't forget the toppings—they are essential to add flavor to this simple meal.*

# french toast

*Prep & cook time: 25 minutes*
*Makes: 2-3 french toasts*
*Difficulty: easy*

1 egg
¼ teaspoon cinnamon
3 tablespoons water or milk
1 tablespoon runny honey
a pinch of salt
¼ teaspoon vanilla extract
2-3 slices sandwich bread, fresh or somewhat stale
1 tablespoon butter
toppings such as honey, jam, maple syrup, or cinnamon and sugar

To begin, make the egg mixture: in your large cooking pot, crack the egg and measure in the cinnamon, water, honey, salt, and vanilla extract. Stir the mixture until it is as blended as possible. Don't worry—it won't look particularly smooth.

Now cook the bread: prime and light your stove, turning it to a low setting. Melt a dab of butter (about a third of a tablespoon) in your frying pan, swirling until the bottom of the pan is coated. Take it off the heat for a moment as you swipe one slice of bread in the egg mixture, flipping it over so that both sides are coated. If you're using stale bread, you'll need to soak it longer.

Place the bread into the frying pan and, holding it an inch or two above the stove, fry the first slice. Flip it halfway through cooking so that both sides end up golden and browned. Slide the cooked french toast onto a plate and cover it with a lid to keep warm. Repeat the process of bread-coating and frying until you've cooked both slices of bread. If you have enough egg mixture left, fry up a third slice.

Serve the French toast with plenty of butter, and your choice of honey, jam, or cinnamon and sugar. Better yet, pour on some real maple syrup.

*It may sound crazy to advocate jam-making on the road, but really it couldn't be easier or more practical. This plummy peach jam recipe can be made in minutes, and can be served on practically anything. If you find yourself with mealy fruit, or specimens that have been bashed and battered from a day on the road, give this recipe a try! Be sure to check out the photo tutorial on page 121 before you begin.*

## plum & peach jam

*Prep & cook time: 15 minutes*
*Makes: about ¾ cup of jam*
*Difficulty: easy*

1 large plum
1 large peach
5 tablespoons sugar
a pinch of salt
½ lemon

Cut the fruit into small chunks, discarding the pits and any rotten spots. Add the chunks to your large cooking pot, along with the sugar and salt. Juice the half of a lemon into the pot, and give the fruit a stir.

Now, get cooking: prime and light your stove, turning it to a low setting. Cook the fruit, stirring constantly as it bubbles, occasionally smooshing some of it gently with the back of your wooden spoon to help them break down a little quicker. After about four or five minutes, when the fruit has mostly dissolved and the fruit is starting to look like a slightly runny, syrupy jam, take it off the heat. It will thicken as it cools to achieve the right jammy consistency.

Once cool, the possibilities are endless. Serve on buttered bread, french toast or crepes. Or, stir it in oatmeal or yogurt. If you don't want to eat it right now, make peanut butter and jam sandwiches to have for lunch or an afternoon snack. Alternatively, put the jam in a sturdy, leak-proof jar, and save it for tomorrow. It should last at least a day or two, depending on the weather.

## JAMMY NOTES:

- Instead of the plum, why not use another peach? Add some minced fresh ginger for a delectable ginger peach jam. Or, add a few drops of almond extract, which goes wonderfully with stone fruits.
- Why not substitute two small plums for the peach? Add cinnamon and Chinese Five Spice for a warm, fall treat.
- When you get the hang of the amount of fruit required, start innovating! Try mango-peach, apricot-nectarine, or strawberry!
- If your jam didn't get thick enough, don't worry. Just try again, and cook it a bit longer next time. In the meantime, call your creation "plummy peach syrup" and drizzle it on crepes. Better yet, mix it with booze for an easy camp cocktail.
- If you want more jam, don't double the recipe. Instead, make separate batches!

You're done when it looks like runny jam!

Crepes with lingonberries above the Arctic Circle in Finland

*I have made these crepes more times than I can count—a plate of them, smeared with soft butter and drizzled with honey, is my very favorite breakfast on the road. I find it sort of miraculous how they come together without any special ingredients, and yet are far more tasty and fancy-looking than one would expect to come out of a rustic camp kitchen! The directions may sound complicated at first, and you may need a couple of tries before mastering the technique, but don't be intimidated. As long as you're armed with a non-stick frying pan, you'll see they're fairly simple. More notes about making these crepes can be found on page 125.*

# browned butter crepes

*Prep & cook time: 30 minutes*
*Makes: 6-7 crepes*
*Difficulty: expert*

2 tablespoons butter, plus more for greasing pan
8 tablespoons flour
1 tablespoon sugar
a pinch of salt
2 eggs
¼ teaspoon vanilla extract
8 tablespoons milk, *or* one 5-oz / 147 ml can of evaporated milk, *or* 8 tablespoons water

Before you do anything else, you're going to do what's called "browning" the butter. It's a simple process that makes regular old butter taste deliciously toasted and nutty. Measure two tablespoons of butter into your frying pan. Prime and light your stove, turning it to a low setting. Hold the pan a couple inches over the flame, and swirl it gently as the butter melts. After it's melted, it will foam a little. Keep swirling, and eventually the butter will begin to turn brown. When it becomes a pale amber color and starts to smell nutty (about two minutes), remove the pan from the heat, and turn off the stove.

As the browned butter cools, prepare the rest of the ingredients: measure the flour, sugar, and salt into your large cooking pot, and stir with a wooden spoon to combine. Next, crack the eggs into the pot and mix well until it's a smooth paste. Stir in the cooled browned butter and vanilla extract, then the milk, water, or evaporated milk.

Get out your large plate and set it near the stove along with your pot lid—they'll come in handy later. Prime and light your stove again, and turn it to a medium-low setting. Add a dab of butter to the frying pan, and let it melt. Then, spoon 3-4 tablespoons of batter into the pan, quickly swirling it to coat the entire surface.

Holding the pan a couple of inches above the stove, move it around so that you're heating a different part of the crepe every five seconds or so. (The goal here is to have an 8-inch crepe cook as evenly as possible over a 3-inch flame—without moving the pan around, you'll end up with a scorched center and gooey edges.)

After about a minute of cooking, the top of the crepe will look a little dry, and the edges of the crepe will release from the pan when you gently push against them with your spatula. Assuming you've used enough butter, a light shake should free the bottom of the crepe from the pan. Now you're ready to flip it: insert your spatula under the crepe, making sure no parts of it are stuck to the pan. Flip it over, and undo any wrinkles or folds. Cook for another minute, or until the crepe takes on some speckled golden splotches.

Transfer the crepe to your large flat serving plate, and cover it with the lid to keep warm. Repeat this process until you run out of batter, greasing your pan with a touch of butter between every third crepe.

## CREPE-Y NOTES:

- As far as toppings go, I prefer jam or honey. Lingonberry preserves are good for Scandinavian flair, and you can't go wrong with a thick smear of Nutella. Why not try a squeeze of lemon juice and a drizzle of honey? How about a sprinkling of cinnamon and sugar?
- On many occasions, I've used olive oil instead of butter in this recipe. The resulting crepes aren't *quite* as tasty as usual, but they're still pretty good. If you do substitute, skip the butter-browning step and simply add two tablespoons of oil to the batter.
- I've also used water in this recipe instead of milk or evaporated milk. The crepes aren't *as* tasty, but they're still good.
- I've even made crepes with both water *and* olive oil. They're passable, but I don't recommend them unless you're desperate.

# SECOND BREAKFAST

Touring cyclists, like hobbits, are food-lovers by nature, and are quick to adopt the idea of eating a second breakfast. And it makes perfect sense—once you've left your campsite and pedalled for an hour or two, you begin to feel a bit peckish. Then, when you start biking past bakeries, markets, and grocery stores, it's nearly impossible not to stop for a mid-morning meal.

Here are a few of my favorite second breakfasts:

- Cold milk and cereal, eaten on stools in front of the grocery store. You'll receive all kinds of strange looks when you park your ragamuffin self by the entryway and consume the entire box in one sitting, but it will be so, so worth it.

- Cold yogurt from a mini-market. I never pass up the chance to have yogurt for my second breakfast, and I keep my spork in my handlebar bag so I'm always at the ready! A bit of honey from the snack pannier is a good addition here.

- Fresh fruit from a roadside stand. If you're lucky, the vendor might take an interest in your journey and offer you a few extra apples or oranges for free.

- Last but certainly not least, a cappuccino and fresh, buttery pastries from a bakery or café. Croissants, strawberry tarts, German chocolate cake... second breakfast doesn't get any better than this!

Pastries from a German bakery for "second breakfast"

*The road from Julierpass to Silvaplana, Switzerland*

# LUNCH
## (AND AFTERNOON SNACKS)

📷 *Lunch in Romania— with a stray dog visitor, of course!*

*This spicy tomato salsa is best when made with juicy, ripe, in-season tomatoes, fresh from the market. Serve with homemade guacamole (page 134) and corn chips from the grocery store.*

# fresh tomato salsa

*Prep time: 15 minutes*
*Makes: 2 servings*
*Difficulty: easy*

2 medium-sized, ripe, juicy tomatoes
¼ onion (about 5 tablespoons, chopped)
1 jalapeño pepper
1 clove garlic
a handful of cilantro
½ lime
½ teaspoon salt
¼ teaspoon black pepper
a pinch of cumin

Chop the tomatoes into small chunks and add them to a large pot or bowl. Mince a quarter of an onion, a clove of garlic, and a jalapeño pepper (removing the seeds for a milder salsa), and add them to the tomatoes. Roughly chop or tear the cilantro leaves and toss them in as well.

Roll the lime on a hard surface to loosen up the juice, and then cut it in half. Juice one half into the tomato mixture, and add the salt, pepper, and cumin. Stir it all together, and eat with chips or tortillas (page 218) for a refreshing lunch.

*Guacamole is so simple it almost doesn't even need a recipe. The idea is to mash up a ripe, buttery avocado with some salt for flavor, and some citrus juice to liven it up. Here, I provide a slightly more flavorful version of this simple spread.*

# guacamole

*Prep time: 10 minutes*
*Makes: 2 servings*
*Difficulty: easy*

2 avocados
1 large garlic clove
a small wedge of onion (1 tablespoon minced)
1 small tomato, chopped
1 tablespoon lemon juice (a generous squeeze)
salt and pepper to taste

Slice the avocados in half around their large central pits. Open the halves, and remove the pits (gently chop your knife into the pit, then twist to dislodge and lift it out). Scoop the flesh of the avocado into a bowl.

Mince the garlic and a thin wedge of onion and add it to the bowl, along with a small tomato chopped into small pieces. Add a squeeze of lemon juice (about a tablespoon), and then mash it all up with a spork or wooden spoon until you have a thick, chunky guacamole dip. Season generously with salt and pepper to taste.

Eat with breakfast burritos (page 108), tortilla chips and salsa (page 133), or smear on a sandwich with turkey and alfalfa sprouts if you can get your hands on some.

*What I love about this lemony bean dip is that it reminds me of hummus. It's an easy way to consume a lot of protein, and there's no need to wash the dishes afterwards, as the can of beans itself becomes its own bowl of dip. White beans seem to be the softest and easiest to smash, but you can give this a shot with any beans you have. Additionally, play with flavors, and season it any way you like.*

# lemony garlic bean spread

*Prep time: 15 minutes*
*Makes: 1 serving*
*Difficulty: easy*

1 16-oz / 425g can of cooked white beans
1 clove garlic
¼ teaspoon paprika
¼ teaspoon salt
¼ teaspoon black pepper
juice of ¼-½ lemon

Open the can of beans and, using its lid as a strainer, drain the liquid. Now, with a wooden spoon, smash the beans in an up-and-down motion, as if using a mortar and pestle. Occasionally scrape the bottom and sides to make sure you're pulverizing everything. It should take about three or four minutes to achieve a fairly smooth consistency.

Mince the clove of garlic and add it to the can along with the paprika, salt, and black pepper. Add lemon juice to taste (I like about half a lemon), and stir to combine. Eat with pita bread, tortillas (page 222), crackers or raw vegetables.

*A flowering Lithuanian field*

Tyler's muddy wheel after a day of riding in Romania

*This summery salad comes together quickly and is utterly delicious as a light lunch or side dish. For assistance preparing the avocado and jalapeño, see "Preparing Your Ingredients" on page 76. Mango help can be found on page 140.*

# mango & avocado salad

*Prep time: 15 minutes*
*Makes: 2 servings*
*Difficulty: easy*

1 avocado
1 mango
1 small wedge red onion (1 tablespoon, minced)
1 jalapeño, seeds removed
¼ teaspoon chili powder
¼ teaspoon chili flakes
Salt and pepper to taste
generous squeeze of lime juice (about half a lime)

First, prepare the fruits: cut the avocado in half and remove the pit. Cut the flesh into a checkerboard pattern and scoop it into a large bowl, separating it into chunks. Slice the mango on each side of the large central pit, then cut each slice into a checkerboard pattern without piercing the skin. Invert the slices and scoop the mango into the bowl as well.

Now, prepare the rest of the salad: mince a thin slice of red onion until you have about a tablespoon. Mince the jalapeño, discarding the seeds. Add both to the bowl along with the chili powder and chili flakes. Season the salad generously with salt, pepper, and lime juice until the flavors sing.

# ⊕ PREPARING A MANGO

1. Cut the mango in thirds, curving outward as you slice to avoid the large central pit.
2. Cut the sides off of the large central pit.
3. Make a checkerboard pattern on each piece of fruit, taking care not to slice through the skin.
4. Invert the slices, and cut the chunks of mango into a bowl. Or, eat them right off the skin!

*I first made this sweet and spicy peanut coleslaw in the Gobi Desert of Mongolia, where mammoth heads of wilty cabbages were the only vegetables available for miles. If you're not in the middle of nowhere in central Asia, you should have a considerably easier time with this.*

# soy peanut cabbage slaw

*Prep time: 15 minutes*
*Makes: 2 heaping bowlfuls of slaw*
*Difficulty: easy*

2 tablespoons sugar
1 tablespoon olive oil
1 teaspoon chili flakes
4 teaspoons soy sauce
½ teaspoon ground, powdered ginger root
½ lemon
¼ medium onion
1 clove garlic
¼ - ½ head of purple or green cabbage
4 heaping tablespoons roasted peanuts
salt and pepper to taste

First get the sauce ready: in your large cooking pot or waterproof basin, measure the sugar, oil, chili flakes, soy sauce, and powdered ginger. Squeeze half a lemon into the container as well (it's no big deal if the seeds fall in), then stir everything to combine.

Now prepare the vegetables: chop the onion into small pieces, and mince the garlic, adding them both to your cooking pot. Now slice your cabbage in half (it could be tough), and then cut out the thick, white heart and discard it. Slice the rest of the cabbage into thin ribbons as best you can, and add them to your two-litre cooking pot until it's about half full. You could use anywhere between a quarter and a half of the cabbage, depending on its size.

Finally, roughly chop or smash (with the flat side of your knife) the peanuts, and toss them in the pot. Stir everything around until the sauce coats all of the vegetables. Season to taste with salt and pepper, and then dig in!

The leftover cabbage should last for another day or two, wrapped in a plastic bag in your pantry pannier. Make another salad tomorrow, or chop it up tonight and make a simple soup out of it. See pages 180-181 for how to invent a soup without a recipe.

# SANDWICH IDEAS

bread or tortilla
+
olive oil or butter
salt
pepper
+
cured meats and/or
cheese slices and/or
tomato slices and/or
cucumber slices and/or
bean spread and/or
tinned fish and/or
lettuce leaves and/or
hard boiled eggs

> To steer this dish in the direction of Italian bread salad, or **panzanella**, cut some good, crusty bread into chunks and toss them with the vegetables. There should be plenty of juice for the bread to soak up.

*We first discovered this salad in Tunisia, where I routinely ordered it in restaurants. We then re-discovered it in Serbia with some added salty cheese under the name "Serbian Salad." I'm fairly certain there are variations on the same theme in Israel and Greece as well, perhaps with some added olives. Flaked tuna from a can would be a typically Tunisian addition, as would a chopped hard boiled egg.*

# salade tunisienne

*Prep time: 15 minutes*
*Makes: 2 servings of salad*
*Difficulty: easy*

2 medium tomatoes
1 medium cucumber
¼ medium onion
1 tablespoon vinegar (any will do)
1 tablespoon olive oil
¾ teaspoon salt
¼ teaspoon pepper

tuna from a can, drained (optional)
hard boiled eggs, chopped (page 159) (optional)
strong, salty cheese, crumbled (optional)
a few cured olives (optional)
fresh, crusty bread (optional)

Cut the tomatoes, cucumber, and onion into roughly uniform chunks, and add them to a large bowl. Add the vinegar, olive oil, salt, and pepper and toss everything together. Top with any optional add-ons you like (or none at all) and serve with fresh, crusty bread if you have some.

*The idea here is to mix and match a veggie or two with black beans, corn, and a simple dressing. It's fresh, easy to prepare, and, paired with some corn chips or bread, makes a satisfying, yet light, meal.*

# black bean summer salad

*Prep time: 15 minutes*
*Makes: 3 generous servings*
*Difficulty: easy*

1 15-oz / 425g can black beans
1 8.5-oz / 241g can of sweet corn kernels
1 bell pepper (orange, yellow, or red)
a wedge of red onion (about 4 tablespoons minced)
1 jalapeño pepper
1 lime
¼ teaspoon ground cumin
¾ teaspoon salt
1 tablespoon runny honey
black pepper, to taste
cilantro, roughly torn or chopped (optional)

Drain the black beans and corn and add them to your large pot. Cut around the stem of the bell pepper and pull it out, discarding the seeds. Chop the pepper into small chunks, and add them to the pot. Mince some onion until you have about 4 loosely packed tablespoons, and add them as well. Cut the jalapeño open, remove the seeds, and mince the pepper finely, adding it to the veggies.

Cut the lime in half and squeeze all of the juice and pulp into the pot. Season with cumin, salt, and honey. Mix everything to combine, then sprinkle on the pepper and torn cilantro.

> For better or worse, I'm pretty lax about washing my greens—if they look clean, I tear them up and use them. However, if you're more stringent than I, this is how to clean your lettuce without suffering through a soggy, sodden salad: rinse leaves with a water bottle until clean, then pat them dry with the cleanest cloth you have. Let them finish drying in the sun while you prepare the dressing. Once dry, they're ready to use.

*This simple way of making salad was taught to me by my host family when I lived in France for a year. You begin by making the dressing in the salad bowl itself, and then add heaps of lettuce and other salad-fixings on top of it. When you toss it, the tiny amount of dressing will be potent enough to flavor everything! Tailor it to suit your tastes: use honey instead of sugar and make "honey mustard" sauce. Use a shallot instead of garlic. Try different vinegars, as they'll all create slightly different flavors.*

# mixed salad with vinaigrette dressing

*Prep time: 15 minutes*
*Makes: two servings of salad*
*Difficulty: easy*

*For the vinaigrette dressing:*
1 large garlic clove
2 tablespoons olive oil
1 teaspoon vinegar (Try red wine, apple cider, or balsamic vinegar. You can even use lemon juice.)
½ teaspoon sugar
1 teaspoon mustard (anything but the neon yellow American-style)
¼ teaspoon salt
¼ teaspoon pepper

*For the salad:*
4 loose cups of torn lettuce leaves or mixed greens (including arugula, baby spinach, etc.)

*Additional optional add-ins:*
- carrot, grated or chopped into small cubes
- red onion, thinly sliced
- sugar snap peas, halved
- radishes, quartered
- bell pepper, sliced and diced
- cucumber, chopped into small cubes
- tomato, chopped
- apple or pear, chopped into small cubes
- mandarin orange segments
- avocado slices
- any kind of cheese, cubed or crumbled
- any kind of cooked or cured meats, chopped
- walnuts, almonds, or pecans, roughly chopped
- raisins or dried cranberries
- hard boiled eggs, quartered (page 159)
- Camp-style croutons (see next page)

First, begin with the dressing: mash the clove of garlic with the flat side of your knife, discard the peel, and mince it finely. Place it in your large cooking pot along with the olive oil, vinegar, sugar, mustard, salt and pepper. Mix everything with your wooden spoon.

Now, make the salad: into your pot or basin, directly atop your little pool of French vinaigrette, add the greens, and any additional add-ins you wish. Toss the salad in the dressing with your wooden spoon until each leaf is lightly coated.

*Though not as crispy as normal baked croutons, these simple chunks of butter-fried bread add delicious flavor to the top of salad or soup. They're pretty addictive though; there may not be any left by the time the meal is ready!*

# camp-style croutons

*Prep & cook time: 10 minutes*
*Makes: 1-2 generous servings*
*Difficulty: easy*

2 slices of bread (fresh or stale)
½ teaspoon garlic granules
¼ teaspoon salt
1 tablespoon butter
1 tablespoon olive oil

First, prepare your ingredients: tear the bread into substantial chunks, and set them in a bowl for later. Measure the garlic granules and salt into a small cup, and set it aside as well. Measure the butter and oil into your frying pan (for a less cramped space, use your large pot if it's not already in use).

Now, get cooking: prime and light your stove, then heat the butter and oil, swirling above the flame, until the butter is melted. Add the bread, and stir everything around until all of the fat is absorbed and the chunks are lightly browned. Sprinkle on the garlic granules and salt, and stir for another moment. Remove the pan from the heat, and toss them onto a soup or salad.

Tyler snacking on a banana in Tunisia

# AFTERNOON SNACKS

On all but the easiest riding days, you're likely going to need an afternoon snack or a post-hill-climb treat. When you're feeling hungry or faint after your lunch is long gone, pull over to the side of the road and open up your snack pannier to see what you've got on hand. Here are a few of my favorite snacking options:

- Fruit and nut granola bar bites (page 156)
- Hard boiled eggs (page 159)
- Chips ("crisps" as our British friends say)
- Crackers & slices of cheese
- Carrots and other easy-to-eat veggies
- Chocolate please, and lots of it!
- Dried fruit and nuts
- Fresh fruit: apples, oranges, and bananas
- Cookies, cookies, cookies!

*Here's a simple version of the classic chewy granola bar that you can easily make at camp using your staples. Simply whip up a batch during the evening, and store them away for the next day's ride. Unless the mixture is completely cool, don't try to add chocolate—it will melt.*

# fruit & nut granola bites

*Prep, cook and wait time: 20 minutes*
*Makes: 10-12 granola bar bites*
*Difficulty: moderate*

10 tablespoons rolled oats
6 generous tablespoons of any combination of chopped nuts, chopped dried fruit, raisins, shredded coconut, or other add-ins
2 tablespoons butter
3 tablespoons honey
2 tablespoons peanut butter
a pinch of salt

First, get the dry ingredients ready: in a cup or bowl, measure the oats and other add-ins such as chopped nuts, chopped dried fruit, raisins, or coconut. Set them aside.

Now, get the wet ingredients cooking: put the butter, honey, peanut butter, and salt into your large cooking pot. Prime and light your stove, and cook the mixture, stirring constantly with a wooden spoon, until it's melted and bubbling.

Add the rest of the ingredients, and then keep stirring for another few seconds until the oats smell lightly toasted. Before they smell *too* much like they're burning, take the pot off the heat and let the mixture cool completely.

Now that the mixture is cool, you have a couple of options. First, if you don't want to get your hands dirty, you can take the loose-but-chewy granola and put it in a bag to munch on later. If you don't mind a little hands-on activity, you can shape the mix by squeezing tablespoonfuls of it into sturdy little balls with the palm of your hand. The more compact they are, the better they will hold up to jostling. Store them in a bag or container, and enjoy during tomorrow's ride.

*Farm-fresh hard boiled eggs are notoriously difficult to peel. A simple trick to make the peels slip right off is to boil a wedge of lemon along with the eggs. Prepare these the night before, so you'll be stocked with healthy, protein-rich snacks for the next day. Be sure to discard them if they develop a funky rotten egg smell.*

# hard boiled eggs

*Prep & cook time: 20 minutes*
*Makes: 6 hard boiled eggs*
*Difficulty: easy*

6 eggs
water for boiling
a slice of lemon (for very fresh eggs)

Place the eggs gently into your large cooking pot, and cover them with cold water until they're submerged. Add the slice of lemon if you're using very fresh eggs.

Prime and light your stove, and crank it up to high heat. Cover the pot of eggs and set it on the flame to cook.

When the water comes to a boil, turn the heat as low as it will go, and let the eggs cook for one minute longer. Remove the pot from the heat altogether, and let it sit for twelve minutes with the lid on. This duration is exact, so be sure to keep track of the time. When twelve minutes have elapsed, drain out the water, and allow the eggs to cool.

Your hard boiled eggs are now ready to roll. Eat throughout the day sprinkled with salt, or serve on a salad (page 151).

Carrots at the market in Da Lat, Vietnam

*A free-camp off the highway in central Italy*

# THE SUPPERTIME FEAST

*I first made this chili when we were cycle touring in Romania. Right before we were ready to call it a night, we stopped at a shop to buy meat and canned goods. Then, we pedaled off in search of a free-camp, which we found shortly after. In an idyllic grove of trees, we made our home for the evening. When the sun began to dip low in the sky, I set about making supper. We cooked and ate the entire pot of this delicious chili, then went to bed to the sounds of dogs barking, insects screeching, and folk music filtering in from some far-off party.*

# chili con carne

*Prep & cook time: 20 minutes*
*Makes: 2-3 generous servings*
*Difficulty: easy*

1 onion
3 cloves garlic
½ pound ground beef
1 teaspoon salt
1 14.5oz / 411g can diced or whole tomatoes
1 15oz /425g can dark red kidney beans
1 6oz / 170g can tomato paste
1 tablespoon chili powder
1 teaspoon cumin
1 teaspoon garlic granules
½ teaspoon chili flakes
½ teaspoon black pepper
¼ teaspoon sugar

First, prepare your ingredients: chop the onion and mince the garlic, then add them to your large cooking pot along with the meat and salt. Open the cans, and get your spice bag and measuring spoons out.

Now, it's time to get cooking: prime and light your cookstove. Sauté the onions and meat over a low flame until the meat is browned and mostly cooked through. Now add the beans (don't drain them), the tomatoes (don't drain them, either), and the tomato paste, stirring to combine. Finally, add the spices and sugar.

Let the chili simmer over low heat for about ten minutes, stirring occasionally. Smash the tomatoes (if whole), and let simmer another few minutes before eating.

*This simple and delicious soup was the very first meal I ever cooked on our two-year adventure. That evening also happened to be my very first foray into the world of free-camping—our tent was pitched on a hidden, daffodil-covered hill just a short day's ride outside of Glasgow, Scotland. I remember hoping that no angry farmer would spot my stove's flame and come yell at me as I nervously sautéed potatoes and leeks. Thankfully, no one ever did. Back then, I made this soup using fresh Scottish cream. Now, I've adapted it to use canned evaporated milk, to make it a bit more convenient. If you have easy access to milk or cream, though, use them!*

# potato leek soup

*Prep & cook time: 30 minutes*
*Makes: 2 generous servings*
*Difficulty: easy*

2 small leeks, or 1 very large one
2 enormous potatoes (Russets would be good here)
2 tablespoons butter
½ teaspoon salt
½ teaspoon pepper
2 teaspoons flour
2 bouillon cubes
24 tablespoons (1½ cups) water
1 12oz / 354ml can evaporated milk, *or* 24 tablespoons (1½ cups) milk, cream, or a combination of the two

First, prepare your ingredients: remove any wilting leaves from the outside of the leek. Cut off and discard the tough, dark-green tops, slicing just above the spot where the leaves start to fan out. Chop off the root end, and discard it as well. Slit the rest of the leek in half lengthwise and examine it for dirt. If you've got a sandy, dirt-filled specimen, fan out the layers slightly and rinse them off with a little water. Once clean, chop the leeks into ¼-inch slices and put them in your large cooking pot.

Next, clean your potatoes as best you can by wiping with a towel or rinsing, and discard any bad spots. Cut the potatoes into small chunks, and add them to the pot. Add the butter, salt, and pepper. Prepare the milk: if using regular milk or cream, measure it into a cup. If using a can of evaporated milk, open it and set it aside.

Now, you can begin cooking: prime and light your stove and sauté the vegetables over a medium flame. Stir often until the leeks are soft, as shown in the photo on page 166. Add the flour, and stir to combine. Remove the pot from the stove so your veggies won't burn, and add the water and bouillon cubes.

Put the pot back on the heat, and allow everything to boil until the potatoes are very tender. When they yield easily to gentle pressure with the back of a spoon, gently smash some of them against the side of the pot. (The smashed potatoes will help thicken the soup.) While you're poking around, make sure the bouillon cubes are completely dissolved.

When the soup has thickened up a bit, and enough potato chunks are smashed to your liking, stir in the milk or cream and simmer for another minute or two before eating.

*This wonderfully simple curry is easy to make, and can be adapted for any season and any mix of vegetables. Whichever ingredients you choose, be sure to have something starchy on hand to sop up the creamy, saucy mixture—this curry is meant to be eaten over a helping of grains (like rice, for instance), or with some bread.*

# potato, carrot & pea curry

*Prep & cook time: 25 minutes*
*Makes: 2-3 generous servings*
*Difficulty: easy*

1 small white or yellow onion
1 large carrot
1 large potato
2 cloves garlic
1 teaspoon salt
½ teaspoon black pepper
2 tablespoons curry powder
¼ teaspoon paprika
¼ teaspoon ground ginger
2 tablespoons butter or olive oil
1 bouillon cube
16 tablespoons (1 cup / 250ml) water
1 13.6oz / 403ml can coconut milk
1 8.5oz / 241g can of peas
squeeze of lemon or lime juice (optional)
rice, other grains, or bread (recommended)

First, prepare your ingredients: chop the onion, carrots, and potatoes into big chunks and add them to your large cooking pot. Mince the garlic, and add it as well. Measure the salt, pepper, curry powder, paprika, and ginger into the pot. Add the butter or olive oil, and the bouillon cube, too.

Shake the can of coconut milk vigorously, then open it and set it aside. Open the can of peas, drain them, and set them aside. Measure out 16 tablespoons of water (1 cup) into a small container, and set it aside.

Now, get started cooking: prime and light your cookstove, turn it to low, and sauté the vegetables and spices for two or three minutes to bring out their flavors. Then, add the water, put the lid on the pot, and let the vegetables boil, cooking until the potatoes and carrots are tender. (Poke them with the tip of your knife once in awhile to check.)

When the fresh vegetables are cooked, add the can of coconut milk and the drained peas. Stir to combine, and heat until the curry is warm again. Season with salt and pepper, and squeeze a little lemon or lime juice on top if you have any. Serve with grains or bread, or eat as-is.

A cozy pot of 'home soup' with Tyler's dumplings, page 174

*Before we left on our world journey, we used to make chicken soup on the weekends. We'd spend Sunday evening in front of the stove, stirring a big pot of homemade chicken broth, to which we'd add cubed potatoes, plenty of onions and garlic, maybe a carrot or two, and whichever herbs and spices sounded good that night. Tyler would make dumplings, and we'd settle in for a cozy winter meal. While on our bike tour, we missed this tradition dearly and would often make this simple, herby broth and call it, fondly, "Home Soup." May it soothe your homesickness, too!*

# a cozy pot of 'home soup' with Tyler's dumplings

*Prep & cook time: 30 minutes*
*Makes: 2 generous servings*
*Difficulty: easy*

For home soup:

    1 enormous potato, such as a Russet
    1 large carrot
    ½ large onion
    3 cloves garlic
    1 tablespoon butter or olive oil
    48 tablespoons (3 cups / 700 ml) of water
    3 chicken bouillon cubes
    ½ teaspoon basil
    ½ teaspoon oregano
    ½ teaspoon rosemary
    ½ teaspoon chili flakes
    ½ teaspoon black pepper
    ¼ teaspoon salt

For Tyler's dumplings:
- 6 tablespoons flour
- 1 egg
- ¼ teaspoon salt
- ½ tablespoon soft butter

First, prepare the soup: chop the potato, carrot, and onion into similar-sized chunks, removing any bad spots. Add them to your large cooking pot. Mince the garlic, and add that as well, along with the butter or olive oil. Prime and light your stove, turn it to low, then sauté the vegetables for a minute. Add the water, bouillon cubes, salt, pepper, and spices, and allow the soup to boil, stirring occasionally.

While the soup is cooking, mix up a batch of Tyler's dumplings: in a small bowl, combine the flour, egg, salt, and butter. Stir until you've got a smooth, sticky, gloppy substance.

When the soup is ready (the vegetables will be very tender and the bouillon cubes completely dissolved, about 20 minutes), drop in small globs of dumpling batter, using your spoon to make sure they don't all stick together. Let the globs cook until they float to the surface. When all of the batter is used and all the dumplings are plump and floating (as shown in the photograph on page 172), dish up and enjoy!

*When making this tomato soup, be sure to add the curry powder, cinnamon, and nutmeg! Though you can't taste the individual herbs and spices in the final product, they layer upon each other in a complex and satisfying way, adding richness, depth, and a whole heap of flavor to what I would normally consider a boring soup. Serve this hearty version with grilled cheese sandwiches (page 183), or with a slice of crusty bread.*

# tomato soup

*Prep & cook time: 20 minutes*
*Makes: 2 servings*
*Difficulty: easy*

½ small onion
1 tablespoon olive oil or butter
¾ teaspoon salt
¼ teaspoon pepper
1 tablespoon flour
1 14.5oz / 411g can crushed or diced tomatoes
a full can's worth of water (about 2 cups)
1 6oz / 170g can tomato paste
2 teaspoons sugar
1 teaspoon basil
½ teaspoon garlic granules
½ teaspoon chili flakes (optional)
¼ teaspoon curry powder
a pinch of cinnamon
a pinch of nutmeg

First, prepare your ingredients: chop the onion into very small pieces, and place it in your large cooking pot along with the oil or butter. Add the salt and pepper. Get out the flour, open cans, and have your water, sugar, and spices ready.

Now, get cooking: set up your stove, prime it, and turn it to a low flame. Sauté the onion until it is semi-translucent and lightly browned around the edges, then add the flour. Stir it in for a minute, until it coats the onions and browns a little. Next, add the can of crushed or diced tomatoes. Fill the can with water, and pour it in, too. Stir in the tomato paste until no lumps remain. Add the sugar, basil, garlic granules, chili flakes, curry powder, cinnamon, and nutmeg. Keep stirring for another few minutes as the soup simmers.

Being careful not to burn your tongue, taste the soup for seasonings, adding sprinklings of salt, pepper, or curry powder if necessary. Serve with bread or a grilled cheese sandwich.

*Thick, savory, and flecked with flashes of vibrant green from the vegetables, this hearty, road-friendly pot-pie stew is the next best thing to the real pastry-topped dish. Some store-bought buttermilk biscuits or soft white rolls served alongside should satisfy cravings for a buttery, flaky pie crust. If you have fresh green beans or peas instead of canned, sauté them in the beginning with the vegetables. If you want to substitute a turnip for the carrot, or play around with other root vegetables besides potatoes, be my guest!*

# hearty pot pie stew

*Prep & cook time: 25 minutes*
*Makes: 2-3 generous servings*
*Difficulty: moderate*

1 carrot
2 medium potatoes, or 1 enormous one
1 onion
3 tablespoons butter
½ teaspoon salt
½ teaspoon ground black pepper
4 tablespoons flour
32 tablespoons (2 cups / 475ml) water
3 bouillon cubes
1 can green beans
½ teaspoon dried thyme
½ teaspoon dried oregano
1 teaspoon garlic granules

First, prepare your ingredients: chop the carrot, potato, and onion into roughly the same size small pieces, and place them in your large cooking pot along with the butter, salt, and pepper. Measure the flour into a small cup, and set it aside. Measure the water into a mug or bowl, and set it aside as well. Open the can of green beans, and drain the liquid, using the lid as a strainer. Set them aside.

Now, get cooking: prime and light your stove, and turn it to low. Sauté the vegetables until the onion is translucent and lightly browned. Add the flour, and stir until everything is dry and clumpy, and the flour has darkened in color. This won't take long.

Next, add the water in thirds, stirring to incorporate it between each addition. Add the bouillon cubes, green beans, thyme, oregano, and garlic granules. Keep cooking, stirring, until all of the vegetables are soft, the bouillon cubes are dissolved, and the stew is thick and creamy.

Serve this chicken-less pot pie stew with crusty bread, or even savory, buttery biscuits if you can get your hands on some. Alternatively, turn it into a calzone (see page 229) by making some dough, stuffing it with the slightly-cooled stew, and frying it up to make a hand-held pot-pie.

## SOUP WITHOUT A RECIPE

Did you know that you don't need a complicated recipe to make soup? All you need is a little practice to get the hang of some basic techniques. With a flexible formula, you can make any number of seasonal soups, using whatever produce you can find.

**Formula for a basic soup:**

1. Add chopped onions, minced garlic, and a tablespoon of butter or oil to your large pot. Sprinkle liberally with salt & pepper, and sauté for a minute.
2. Add any other chopped vegetables, and sauté them for a bit, too.
3. Add bouillon cubes and water.
4. Add plenty of spices and herbs of your choice.
5. Let everything simmer/boil until mostly tender.
6. Add any leafy greens or quick-cooking vegetables.
7. Remove from heat. Taste your creation, and adjust seasonings as necessary.

**Ideas for making a heartier soup:**

- Add some chopped potatoes in Step 2. When they are very tender (Step 5), smash them with the back of your wooden spoon.
- Mix a tablespoon of flour with a tablespoon of water in a small cup, making sure there aren't any lumps. Add the mixture to the soup at Step 5 or 6, and let simmer.
- Add torn-up bits of fresh or stale bread at any point during the cooking process. When they are soft, break them up with your wooden spoon.
- At Step 1, add a tablespoon of flour to the onions, garlic, and butter, stirring until it becomes a thick paste. When it browns lightly, add the water in splashes, stirring in between each addition.
- Add milk or cream instead of some of the water.
- Add some dry pasta, rice, lentils or quinoa, along with the water in Step 3. Be sure to cook the soup until the pasta/grains are tender.
- Add some cheese at Step 6, and allow it to melt.
- Add meat, sautéing it with the onions in Step 1, or with the chopped vegetables in Step 2.

> For some variation, why not try a different kind of cheese, such as mozzarella? Or, how about skipping the garlic, and spreading one slice of bread with apricot, fig, or plum jam before putting the cheese on. Very thin apple or pear **slices** added to the cheese layer would be delicious. Alternatively, why not spread a thin layer of harissa, hot sauce, or basil pesto on the inside of your bread slices?

*Tyler makes the best grilled cheese sandwiches of anybody I know. I'm more than happy to sit back and relax while he prepares his signature version of them for me! He advises using real cheddar cheese, and says not to omit the salt and garlic sprinkle.*

# Tyler's grilled cheese

*Prep & cook time: 15 minutes*
*Makes: 1 grilled cheese sandwich*
*Difficulty: easy*

2 slices bread
1½ oz / 42g cheddar cheese
1 tablespoon soft butter
salt and garlic granules

Spread a half-tablespoon of butter onto each slice of bread. Sprinkle them each with a small pinch of salt and a generous pinches of garlic granules. Place one slice in your frying pan, buttered side down. Slice the cheddar into thin sheets, and lay them evenly on top of the bread. Place the second slice of bread on the cheese layer, buttered side facing upwards.

Prime and light your stove, and turn it to low. Holding the pan a couple of inches above the flame, fry the sandwich for a minute or two, *covered*. Lift the lid to take a peek—when the cheese begins to soften, and a glance underneath the bread reveals a golden brown bottom, carefully flip the sandwich. Then, put the lid back on, and fry until the second side is golden brown, too. Serve with tomato soup (page 176), or simply as is.

## PASTA TIPS:

- Always add salt to pasta water; it will give the bland starch a little flavor. That being said, I don't recommend boiling pasta in seawater. Trust me, I've tried it! Tyler and I both love salt, but even we couldn't handle the salinity.
- Stir the pasta when you put it in the pot so it doesn't all stick together in a big glob.
- Never cook pasta with the lid on, or your pot will foam up and boil over, and you don't really want that to happen. (Though it's not the end of the world if it does.)
- Remember to take a break from whatever ingredients you're preparing so that you can check your pasta for doneness from time to time. You want the noodles to be tender and pleasant to eat—not too soft, not too hard.
- Take great care when straining pasta. I've lost many a pot of noodles when I lose my grip on the strainer lid and my pasta comes tumbling onto the ground. If that happens to you, try not to get *too* upset. Salvage the pasta you can, and move on.

*This deliciously indulgent dish of noodles with caramelized cheese and garlic is the meal we make most often when we're on the road. We've made it on the beaches of Crete, in the fields of Serbia, and even while camped under an Italian bridge. Definitely make it if you love garlic and cheese as much as we do! Just a warning, though: you absolutely need a non-stick pot to make this.*

# our very favorite cheesy garlic pasta

*Prep & cook time: 30 minutes*
*Makes: 2 generous servings*
*Difficulty: easy*

½ pound (8oz / 227g) rigatone or penne pasta
water for boiling
1 teaspoon salt for the pasta water
5 large, firm cloves of garlic
½ teaspoon garlic granules
½ teaspoon salt for seasoning
3 tablespoons olive oil
2oz / 58g good parmesan (or other salty, strong-flavored cheese)
2oz / 58g mozzarella (or other melty, stringy cheese)

First, cook the pasta: fill your large cooking pot with water, and add a teaspoon of salt. Prime and light your cookstove, crank it up to high heat, and set the pot on it to boil.

While waiting for the water to heat, get out your pasta. When the water comes to a boil, add the noodles and stir them so they won't stick to one another. Let them cook, uncovered.

While the pasta is cooking, prepare the other ingredients: mince the garlic cloves and add them to your frying pan. Add the garlic granules, salt, and olive oil. Cut the cheeses into small pieces, and set them aside.

Check on your noodles. When they're tender, drain them, and set the large pot aside. Transfer the cookset handle to your frying pan.

Holding the pan a few inches above a low flame, fry the garlic, swirling or stirring occasionally so it cooks evenly, until it's a deep golden brown color. *Don't let the garlic burn—if it turns black, the flavor will be bitter and you'll have to throw it out and start over.*

Pour the browned garlic and oil mixture over the pasta, and toss in the cheese chunks. Switch your cookset handle to the large pasta pot, and set it on the stove. Stir everything to combine.

Now, you're going to caramelize the cheesy pasta: making sure some of the hunks of cheese are touching the bottom, let the pot sit on the flame without stirring it. After a minute or so, scrape the bottom of the pan with your wooden spoon and rotate the noodles, flipping them over so that a different batch of cheese chunks can caramelize and brown.

Repeat the flipping process as many times as you like, until delicious browned cheese chunks are liberally strewn about the pasta. Some noodles will be crusty, while others will be soft. Serve with bread, or vegetables if you're feeling healthy.

Our very favorite cheesy garlic pasta (page 186)

Rice noodles with stir-fried broccoli and onion (page 190)

*I've created many variations of this simple stir-fry over time, which I've streamlined into this version. Still-crunchy broccoli in a savory soy sauce tossed in a tangle of rice noodles… what's not to love? I like to use broccoli, but you could also use kai-lan (Chinese broccoli) or green beans.*

# rice noodles with stir-fried broccoli and onion

*Prep & cook time: 30 minutes*
*Makes: 2-3 servings*
*Difficulty: expert*

3.5oz / 100g thin rice noodles
water for boiling
1 medium onion
2 cloves garlic
1 small head of broccoli (or half of a large head)
2 tablespoons sugar
3 tablespoons olive oil
½ teaspoon chili flakes
½ teaspoon black pepper
½ teaspoon salt
½ teaspoon powdered ginger
3 tablespoons soy sauce

Fill your large pot nearly full of water, and cover it with the lid. Prime and light your cookstove, crank it up to high heat, and set the water on the flame to heat.

While you're waiting for the water to boil, begin preparing your ingredients: chop the onion into large chunks and mince the garlic on your large cutting board. (Save your large plate for later). Set these aside, and check on your water.

When the water has come to a boil, turn off the stove and take the pot off the flame. Add the noodles to the pot, broken in half so they fit. Put the lid on, and set aside for 8-10 minutes so they can soften. **Note**: *the width of your particular rice noodles will affect the amount of time they'll need to soak. Taste them to judge their tenderness instead of relying solely on the number of minutes.*

While the noodles are softening, make room on your cutting board to chop the broccoli. Cut the end off the broccoli's stem and discard it, then chop the broccoli (both stem and florets) into chunks.

When the noodles are tender, drain them, taking care not to accidentally dump the entire pot in the grass. Transfer the noodles to a wide plate, and cover with a lid to keep warm.

Into the now-empty pot, add the sugar, olive oil, chili flakes, black pepper, salt, and powdered ginger. Give those a quick stir, then add the onion, garlic, and broccoli. Prime and light your stove once more, turn it to medium-low heat, and sauté the vegetables, stirring to mix all of the ingredients. You want to cook the vegetables until the onions are brown in places, and the broccoli is still a bit crunchy.

Add the soy sauce, and stir until everything is combined. Finally, add the pasta into the sauce, teasing it apart if it's stuck together, stirring to coat the noodles completely. When the pasta is warm, you're ready to eat.

Cooking an Italian feast on the island of Elba

*With the help of your spice bag, it's easy to create a delicious Italian feast on the road! I've made this pasta dish on many occasions, but my favorite was when we were stealth-camping on a concrete slab on Italy's famous Amalfi coast. (The photo of our free-camp can be found on page 274.) What a simple way to revel in the delights of such a luxurious location!*

# spaghetti marinara

*Prep & cook time: 20 minutes*
*Makes: 2-3 generous servings*
*Difficulty: easy*

½ pound (8oz / 227g) spaghetti noodles
water for boiling
1 teaspoon salt for the pasta water
½ onion
2 garlic cloves
1 tablespoon butter or olive oil
½ teaspoon dried basil
¾ teaspoon dried oregano
½ teaspoon garlic powder
¾ teaspoon salt
¼ teaspoon ground black pepper
1 teaspoon sugar
1 6oz / 170g can tomato paste
a tomato paste can full of water (¾ cup / 177 ml)
parmesan cheese (optional)
chili flakes (optional)

First, cook the pasta: fill your large cooking pot with water, and add a teaspoon of salt. Prime and light your stove, and turn it to a high setting. Cover the pot, and set it on the stove.

While you're waiting for water to heat, grab the bundle of spaghetti with two hands and break it in half. When the water comes to a boil, remove the lid and add your pasta, stirring so the noodles don't stick to one another.

Let the pasta cook, uncovered, while you prepare the ingredients for the marinara sauce. Chop the onion and mince the garlic, adding them to your frying pan. Now add the butter or olive oil, and the basil, oregano, garlic powder, salt, pepper, and sugar. Open your can of tomato paste and set it aside. Make sure you have a water bottle on hand.

Test the noodles for doneness, and when they are tender, take them off the heat and turn down the stove to a low flame. Drain the pasta over any dirty dishes you have, or into the grass, and set it aside. Cover it with a lid to keep the heat in.

Now, get started with the sauce. Transfer the cookset handle to your frying pan, and heat the onion mixture over a low flame, stirring constantly to melt the butter (if using). When the onions are cooked and beginning to look a bit translucent, add the tomato paste. Fill the tomato paste can with water, and add that, too. Stir gently until everything is smooth, and heat the mixture until it simmers. Remove the pan from the stove and set it aside.

To serve, spoon the marinara sauce over the pasta. Slice some good parmesan cheese as thinly as you can, and toss it on top. Sprinkle on some chili flakes, too, if you love them as much as we do.

*This refreshing noodle dish isn't even remotely authentic, but to me, it is the American cousin of Pad Thai. The first time I made it, I was sitting on the beaches of Crete watching waves roll in and out. As I minced onion and soaked noodles, a drippy-haired surfer emerged from the water and walked over to our camp. Thus, we met Dimitri, a traveler who was living on Crete for the sole purpose of surfing. We invited him to join us the next day for a tour of the famed Dikteon Andron cave, but he declined, shaking his head and shrugging his shoulders as if he had no choice in the matter. "Can't, dude. **Surf**."*

# sweet-spicy peanut noodles

*Prep & cook time: 25 minutes*
*Makes: 2 generous servings*
*Difficulty: moderate*

7oz / 200g thin rice noodles
water for boiling
¼ of a small onion (5 tablespoons, minced)
2 cloves garlic
3 tablespoons sugar
2 tablespoon soy sauce
1 lime
4 tablespoons crunchy peanut butter
½ teaspoon dried chili flakes
additional wedge of lime, optional
scallion (green onion), optional

Fill your large pot nearly full of water, and cover it with a lid. Prime and light your cookstove, and crank it up to a high heat, setting your pot on the flame. While you're waiting for the water to boil, measure out your rice noodles and break them in half so they'll fit in the pot.

When the water has come to a boil, turn off the stove and take the pot off the flame. Add the noodles and put the lid on, setting them aside for 8-10 minutes so they can soften. ***Note****: the width of your particular rice noodles will affect the amount of time they'll need to soak. Taste them to judge their tenderness instead of relying solely on the number of minutes.*

As the noodles soften, chop the onion into very small pieces, and mince the garlic. Set the cutting board aside, and begin preparing the sauce.

Into a small bowl, measure the sugar and soy sauce. Roll the lime on the ground or between your two hands to release its juices, then cut it in half, and juice it into the bowl. Add the peanut butter and chili flakes. Stir until everything is smoothly incorporated.

*As you prepare the sauce, remember to keep an eye on the noodles, taste-testing them to determine doneness. When they're tender and easy to eat, strain out the water and set them aside.*

When the sauce is finished and the cooked pasta is strained, it's time to assemble the dish. Add the onion, garlic, and sauce to the pot, and stir gently until the noodles are coated. Serve with an additional slice of lime and a minced scallion.

*My favorite version of this versatile pasta dish features extra-sharp cheddar and elbow noodles to make the American classic: macaroni and cheese. You could just as easily make alfredo, though, by using fettuccini noodles and good parmesan cheese. Why not try a blue cheese pasta? Or how about a four-cheese pasta to use up the final bits of cheeses you have on hand? For extra decadence, why not add some sliced bacon, cooking it with the onions?*

# pasta in creamy, choose-your-own cheese sauce

*Prep & cook time: 25 minutes*
*Makes: 2-3 generous servings*
*Difficulty: moderate*

½ pound (8oz / 227g) pasta (any shape will do)
water for boiling
1 teaspoon salt for the pasta water
½ a medium onion
2 tablespoons butter
¼ teaspoon pepper
½ teaspoon salt
4 teaspoons flour
1 12oz / 354g can of evaporated milk, or 24 tablespoons (1½ cups) whole milk
4oz / 113g salty, strong-flavored cheese
garlic granules & chili flakes for sprinkling

First, cook the pasta: fill your large cooking pot with water, and add a teaspoon of salt. Prime and light your stove, and turn it to a high setting. Cover the pot, and set it on the stove. When the water comes to a boil, remove the lid and add your pasta, stirring so the noodles don't stick to one another. Let cook, uncovered.

As you're waiting for the pasta to become tender, get your cheese sauce preparations underway: mince the onion, and set it in a small bowl along with the butter, pepper, and ½ teaspoon salt. Cut the cheese into thin slices and set them aside. Open the can of evaporated milk, but don't do anything with it yet.

When the pasta is cooked, take it off the stove and turn the flame down to low. Strain the pasta, then transfer it to a large rimmed plate and cover it with a lid to keep warm.

Now, it's sauce-making time: to the large pot, add the onions, butter, pepper, and salt. Sauté the onions over low heat until they are lightly browned and semi-translucent. Add the flour, stirring quickly until it's evenly dispersed throughout the onions. Add the milk in thirds, stirring constantly between each addition to allow the mixture to thicken and bubble a bit.

When all of the liquid is incorporated, add the cheese and stir until it's melted. Add the cooked noodles, and stir to coat them with sauce. When the pasta has warmed up again, you're ready to eat. Sprinkle each portion liberally with salt, garlic granules and chili flakes.

*Creamy, warm and comforting, this tuna casserole is sure to become a favorite go-to meal, especially for those traveling in groups of three or four. This recipe makes a large quantity of food, so be sure you're hungry! For a crispy finish, top with crumbled potato chips or some crunchy fried onions, found at Asian markets or in the salad-dressing aisle of American supermarkets.*

# camper's tuna casserole

*Prep & cook time: 25 minutes*
*Makes: 3-4 generous servings*
*Difficulty: moderate*

½ pound (8oz / 227g) wide egg noodles
1 teaspoon salt for the pasta water
water for boiling
2 tablespoons butter
½ large onion
½ teaspoon salt
½ teaspoon pepper
2 tablespoons flour
1 12oz / 354ml can of evaporated milk, or 24 tablespoons (1½ cups) whole milk
4oz / 115g cheddar cheese
2 5oz / 142g cans of tuna
1 8.5oz / 241g can of peas
potato chips (crisps) or crispy fried onions (optional)

First, get some water boiling: fill your pot with water, and a teaspoon of salt. Prime and light your cookstove, crank it up to high, and bring the pot of water to a boil.

As the water is heating, prepare your ingredients: mince the onion, and set it aside in a small bowl. Get the flour, salt, and pepper out, and get your measuring spoons at hand.

When the water is boiling, add the pasta and let it cook, uncovered, until it's tender. As it cooks, continue preparing the rest of the ingredients: cut the cheddar into thin slices. Open and drain the cans of tuna and peas, using their lids as strainers. Shake the can of evaporated milk vigorously, then open it up. Give the pasta a stir now and then, taste-testing a noodle or two for doneness.

When the pasta is tender, drain it and transfer to a large plate, resting a lid on top to keep it warm. Set it aside, and turn the stove down to a low setting.

Now, make the sauce: in the large cooking pot, add the butter and chopped onion, along with the salt and pepper. Stir for about five minutes until the butter is melted and the onion is cooked through. Then, add the flour, stirring until it coats the onions and has browned slightly.

Add the milk in two additions, stirring constantly between each one to allow the mixture to thicken and bubble a bit. Add the cheese, and stir to melt it. Finally, toss in the pasta, tuna, and peas. Stir gently until everything is warm. Serve with crumbled potato chips or crispy fried onions.

*Introduced to us by our German friends, Felix and Nadine, this Berlin street food classic quickly became one of our favorite meals to cook on the road. Curry powder, ketchup, and a little heat from cayenne pepper make for a surprisingly addictive combination, especially when paired with really good bratwurst or sausage.*

# berlin-style currywurst

*Prep & cook time: 15 minutes*
*Makes: 2-3 servings*
*Difficulty: easy*

8 tablespoons (½ cup) ketchup
1 teaspoon paprika
1 teaspoon onion powder
2 teaspoons curry powder, plus extra for garnish
cayenne pepper (optional)
2 tablespoons water
1 package pre-cooked bratwurst (4-6 sausages)

First, prepare the sauce: mix the ketchup, paprika, onion powder, curry powder, and water in a small bowl.

Now, cook the bratwurst: prime and light your cookstove, and turn it to low. Place the brats in your frying pan or large cooking pot, and set them on the stove to warm up. When the brats are hot and blistering, remove them from the heat.

Slice the bratwurst into rounds and dollop the sauce on top. Sprinkle on some extra curry powder for color, and some cayenne pepper for heat.

*I first made this hearty meat and potato supper, vaguely reminiscent of the French alpine dish 'tartiflette,' as we were cycling across Italy in the middle of January. Speck, a juniper-smoked cured meat, is the star of the show in this rich dish. Unless you're in Italy, however, it will likely be costly and difficult to track down. Instead, substitute bacon, or some other smoky cured meat. Just a warning: you absolutely need a non-stick pot to make this dish. To see a photo of the finished product, check out pages 208-209.*

# hearty meat & potatoes for a cold winter's night

*Prep & cook time: 25 minutes*
*Makes: 2 generous servings*
*Difficulty: moderate*

5-6 small potatoes, or 2-3 large baking potatoes
4-5 slices speck, bacon ("streaky bacon"), or smoky cured meat of your choosing
2 tablespoons butter (just 1 if using bacon)
½ teaspoon salt
½ teaspoon pepper
½ medium onion
4oz / 113g smoked Gouda, or any other strong cheese you happen to have on hand
garlic granules (optional)

First prepare your ingredients: peel the potatoes if you wish (I never do) and cut off any bad spots. Slice them into thin rounds. Chop the meat into postage-stamp-sized pieces. Add the potatoes and meat to your large cooking pot, along with the butter, salt, and pepper.

Cut the cheese and the onion into medium-sized chunks, and set them aside.

Now, cook the potatoes: prime and light your stove, and turn it to the lowest setting. Sauté the potatoes and meat, stirring and separating the potato slices, until the potatoes are mostly cooked, about 7 minutes. Add the cheese and onions, stirring, until the cheese melts and the onions are cooked.

Next, flatten the mound of potato slices as best you can. Leave them alone for a minute or two without stirring, or until the cheese on the bottom browns and caramelizes, creating a delicious crusty layer. Flip the mass of potatoes over in two or three chunks, and allow the potatoes and cheese to caramelize on the second side.

When nearly everything is golden and crusty, turn off the stove, and allow the potatoes to cool slightly. Serve straight from the pot, sprinkled liberally with garlic granules and more black pepper.

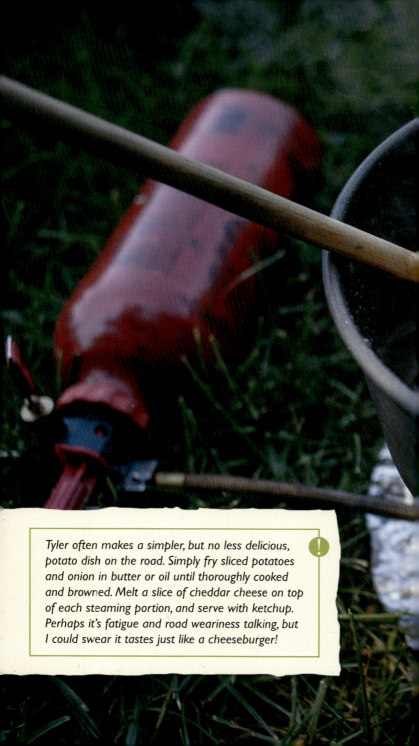

*Tyler often makes a simpler, but no less delicious, potato dish on the road. Simply fry sliced potatoes and onion in butter or oil until thoroughly cooked and browned. Melt a slice of cheddar cheese on top of each steaming portion, and serve with ketchup. Perhaps it's fatigue and road weariness talking, but I could swear it tastes just like a cheeseburger!*

Hearty meat and potatoes for a cold winter's night, page 206

*I'm not sure there's anything more deliciously comforting and homey than a big pot of buttery crushed potatoes, awash in a sea of gravy. Reserve this dish for your coldest, most homesick evenings. For gravy assistance, see the photos on pages 212-213.*

# smashed potatoes & gravy

*Prep & cook time: 30 minutes*
*Makes: 2 generous, rich helpings*
*Difficulty: moderate*

4 large, starchy potatoes such as Russets
water for boiling
1½ teaspoons salt
2 tablespoons butter for the gravy
2 tablespoons flour
2 bouillon cubes or 2 teaspoons bouillon granules
16 tablespoons (1 cup) water for the gravy
3 tablespoons butter for the potatoes
¼ teaspoon garlic granules
salt, black pepper, and garlic granules to taste

First, prepare the potatoes: peel them if you wish (I never do), remove any bad spots, and cut them into small chunks. Put the chunks into your large pot along with the salt and enough water to amply cover everything. Prime and light your stove, and crank it up to high. Set the pot on the stove, and leave the potatoes to boil, uncovered.

While the potatoes are cooking, prepare the rest of the ingredients: for the gravy, put 2 tablespoons of butter and 2 tablespoons of flour into your frying pan. Using a knife on your cutting board, shave the bouillon cubes into a fine powder, and add them to the frying pan, too. Measure the water for the gravy into a cup and set it aside.

Now, back to the potatoes. When you can smash a piece very easily with the back of your wooden spoon, it's done. Please don't break your spoon, and please don't send a burning hot potato chunk flying into your eye by *forcing* it. (I'm speaking from experience here)—when they are ready, it will be *easy*.

When the potatoes are easy to smash, turn off your stove and take the pot off the flame. Strain the water into a bowl, but don't do a thorough job of it. Leave a little puddle in the bottom of the pan—it should be easy to see when you tilt the pot, but not when you set it flat. Reserve the bowl of strained liquid for later.

Before the potatoes cool down, add 3 tablespoons of butter and the garlic granules, and then begin smashing the potatoes with your wooden spoon against the sides of the pot. When you're left with creamy, slightly lumpy mashed potatoes, you're done. If the potatoes aren't creamy enough, you can always add another tablespoon or two of hot potato water, and mix it in. Put the lid on, and set the potatoes aside.

Now, for the gravy. First, check out the "hop on the gravy train" section on page 212. When you're ready to get started, light your stove again, and turn it to a low setting. Put your frying pan on the flame, and melt the butter while mixing it with the flour, stirring carefully and quickly until it's a bubbly paste. Add the cup of plain water (don't use the leftover potato water, as it's too salty and too starchy) by thirds, mixing thoroughly after each addition. Stir until everything has melded into a creamy gravy. Pour the gravy over the potatoes, season liberally with black pepper and garlic granules, and enjoy, straight from the pot.

## HOP ON THE GRAVY TRAIN:

It is my firm belief that everyone should know how to make a simple butter and flour based sauce, whether at home or on the road. You'll get the hang of this easy technique when making several recipes in this book, from gravies to cream sauces. Here's the cooking process in action, broken down visually:

1. Melt a bit of butter and stir in some flour, mixing until it browns a little. This is called the **roux**, pronounced "roo."
2. Now, add a splash of liquid—this could be water, milk, or a savory broth.
3. Mix until you smooth out the lumps, making everything creamy.
4. When the mixture starts to look dry again, as it does in photo on the left, add more liquid.
5. Repeat the stirring and liquid-adding until you've created a velvety, creamy sauce, as shown below.

*Frying can be messy and annoying, but this recipe for zucchini feta fritters is just too good to pass up! Read up on my helpful frying tips (pages 216-217) before you attempt these, and check out the photo, too, so you know what you're aiming for. These fritters are packed full of flavor—don't substitute a different kind of cheese for the feta in this dish, unless it is very salty and strong.*

# zucchini feta fritters

*Prep & cook time: 30 minutes*
*Makes: 15-17 fritters*
*Difficulty: expert*

1 small (6 - 7 in / 15-18 cm long, thin) zucchini
¼ onion
1 large garlic clove
2oz / 57g feta cheese, crumbled
1 tablespoon lemon juice
¼ teaspoon black pepper
¼ teaspoon chili flakes
½ teaspoon salt
2 eggs
3 tablespoons flour
oil for frying, about 2-3 tablespoons (I always use olive oil, but you can use something with a higher smoke point, if you wish)
Greek yogurt or sour cream for serving (optional)

First, prepare your ingredients: cut off the ends and any bad spots of the zucchini. Chop it and the quarter of an onion into chunks the size of corn kernels or smaller. *(If the chunks are too big, the fritters won't hold together.)* Add them to your large cooking pot. Mince the garlic and add it, too. Toss in the crumbled feta cheese, and add the lemon juice, pepper, chili flakes, and salt. Finally, crack in the eggs and add the flour. Mix with a wooden spoon to combine.

Now, get cooking: pour about 1 tablespoon of oil into your frying pan. Prime and light your cook stove, and turn it to a low setting. Hold the pan above the flame, and watch it carefully. When the oil begins to shimmer, and a droplet of water will sizzle and sputter when flicked in it, you're ready to fry.

Taking the pan off the stove for a moment, spoon the zucchini mixture by the tablespoonful (not heaping) into the hot oil. *Don't try to fry more than four at a time.*

Holding the pan over the stove again, swirl it gently so that the oil evenly runs between the fritters. Move the pan around so that each fritter on your roughly 8" frying pan has a chance to cook evenly on your roughly 3" burner. *The oil will sputter, so take care not to burn yourself.*

When the fritters are a dark golden brown on the underside (check with your spatula), flip them over carefully. When the second sides are dark golden brown, too, transfer them to a plate. Continue making fritters in this same manner, adding a little oil to your pan as necessary, until all of the zucchini mixture is cooked.

Enjoy the fritters as-is, or top them with a dollop of sour cream or Greek yogurt, if you happen to have any.

# I BELIEVE I CAN FRY

Frying food on the road can take some getting used to. Hot, sputtering oil and an open flame are enough to make anyone nervous! However, don't let a fear of frying prevent you from exploring the wonderful world of greasy food. To help you along the way, here are some tips to make your fritter creation a success:

- Give the zucchini mixture a stir now and then, so you're sure to have some flour and egg (the ingredients that hold them together) in each spoonful.
- When cooking, hold the pan a couple of inches above the flame so you don't scorch anything, Swirl the pan gently so that each fritter gets some time directly over the flame.
- Take the pan off the heat when you're adding the next round of zucchini mixture to the oil. Never let an empty pan (or a pan of oil) sit on the stove without a hand and a watchful eye on it.
- Add a bit more oil if your pan is getting dry. I've usually added another tablespoon by the time I'm done frying the fritters.

Zucchini feta fritters, page 214

*My favorite way of preparing vegetables is this ridiculously simple technique: I sauté whatever veggie I have on hand in a bit of olive oil, and add a hefty amount of minced garlic. This version features fresh green beans, and a final sprinkling of garlic granules that sends this dish over the top.*

# garlicky green beans

*Prep & cook time: 15 minutes*
*Makes: 2 large side-dish portions*
*Difficulty: easy*

about ½ pound (8oz / 226g) green beans
4 cloves garlic
1 tablespoon olive oil
¼ teaspoon salt
¼ teaspoon pepper
garlic granules

First, prepare your ingredients: snap or cut the stem ends off the green beans. Slice the beans into halves or thirds, and add them to your large cooking pot. Mince the garlic and add it, too. Finally, measure in the olive oil, salt, and pepper, and give the beans a stir.

Now, you're ready to cook: prime and light your stove, turning it to the lowest setting. Sauté the green beans for about three minutes, or until they're semi-cooked but still a bit crunchy, with a few browned spots on the outside. Sprinkle with garlic granules, and enjoy.

> ❗ You really can't go wrong with garlic, olive oil, and a good sprinkling of garlic granules. Try cooking any fresh, in-season vegetable this way, and you'll see how easy it is to create truly delicious food!

# FUN WITH DOUGH

Dough-making may seem too laborious for a traveling cyclist, but I assure you it isn't. Armed with enthusiasm, patience, and water for cleaning up, you're ready to tackle the recipes on the following pages, and taste the most delicious camp food you've ever had! Here are some tips to get you started:

- Get your large plate and cutting board out—they'll be your countertops and work spaces.
- The amount of water and flour you'll need is largely dependent upon the humidity in your area. The dough should be soft and springy, and should hold together. If yours is too wet and gooey, add a little flour to your hands and your workspace.
- To roll out the dough, use whatever you can find: a tin can, a bottle of olive oil, or your hands!
- If you develop holes or tears in your dough, you can repair them easily with a patch of dough "glued" on with a bit of water.
- To clean your hands, simply rub your palms together vigorously until the dried dough peels off.

*We were camping in France when we developed a mad craving for soft tacos. The only problem was, we couldn't find any good tortillas! So, Tyler decided we could make our own, and looked up how to do it. With a bit of flour, water, and salt, we were in business. Our very first tortilla-making session was a success, and opened up a whole new world of dough-related camp cooking. Thanks, honey!*

# Tyler's tortillas

*Prep & cook time: 30 minutes*
*Makes: 4 8-inch tortillas*
*Difficulty: expert*

16 tablespoons (1 cup) flour
½ teaspoon salt
enough water to form a dough (about 8 tablespoons)

First, make the dough: into your large non-stick cooking pot, measure the flour and salt, and combine it with your wooden spoon. Then, add water and stir until you're able to combine everything into a rough-looking dough. With floured fingers, squish the ball of dough in your hands, turning and squashing until it becomes smoother, and of a more uniform consistency. The dough should not be overly sticky, so be sure to add a bit more flour if it is.

Tear the lightly-kneaded dough into four equal chunks. Take the first piece and place it on your large cutting board. Flatten it with your fingers, then take a can of beans (or a bottle of olive oil, or whatever you can find) to it, rolling until the dough is very thin, and slightly smaller than the size of your skillet. Set the tortilla aside on your large plate, and proceed in the same manner with the other hunks, finding room for the tortillas where you can. You can stack them on top of one another, but be sure to dust them liberally with flour first so they don't stick together. When all of your flattened dough hunks are ready, tidy up, and set up your cookset.

Now, it's time to get cooking: prime and light your stove, turn it to a low flame, and get your non-stick frying pan ready. Place a flattened round of dough into your pan (don't add oil, butter, or anything but the dough), and hold it about an inch above the flame. Move the pan around so that your roughly 8" tortilla can cook evenly on your small burner.

Use your spatula to check the tortilla—when the underside is no longer doughy, and is splotched with crusty black charred spots, you're ready to flip. Allow the second side to cook until it, too, is splotchy. Transfer the finished tortilla to a plate, and use the same technique to cook the rest. Serve wrapped around spicy scrambled eggs (page 108), or with anything, really—the presence of a warm, chewy tortilla turns any humble meal into a feast.

*Making simple flatbreads while camped in Romania*

*There is nothing like tearing into one of these hot, greasy, deliciously spiced flatbreads when you're tired and ravenous. As is the case with all of my favorite road-friendly recipes, this one is fairly basic, and requires very few ingredients besides the pantry items already lurking in your panniers. Before you begin, read up on dough-making (page 221), and bear in mind: to make this recipe in the easiest possible way, you'll need two flat "countertops"—a large plate and a cutting board work nicely.*

# rosemary flatbread with garlic and chili flakes

*Prep & cook time: 30 minutes*
*Makes: 2 flatbreads*
*Difficulty: expert*

8 tablespoons (½ cup) flour
¼ teaspoon salt for the dough
about 4 tablespoons (¼ cup) water
½ teaspoon garlic granules or powder
½ teaspoon rosemary leaves
½ teaspoon chili flakes
¼ teaspoon salt for the topping
1 tablespoon olive oil for the topping
4 teaspoons oil for frying

First, make the dough: into your large non-stick cooking pot, measure the flour and ¼ teaspoon salt, and mix it up with your wooden spoon. Then, add water and stir until you're able to combine everything into a rough-looking dough. With floured fingers, squish the ball of dough in your hands, turning and squashing until it becomes smoother, and of a more uniform consistency. The dough should not be overly sticky, so be sure to add a bit more flour if it is.

Tear the lightly-kneaded dough into two equal chunks. Take the first piece and place it on your large cutting board. Flatten it with your fingers, then take a can of beans (or a bottle of olive oil, or whatever you can find) to it, rolling until the dough is thin, and just smaller than the size of your pan.

Next, roll out your second flatbread in the same manner as the first, this time using your large plate as a "countertop." When you're done rolling out both pieces of dough, tidy up a bit and set up your cookset.

Now, make the herb topping. Measure the garlic granules, rosemary leaves, chili flakes, and ¼ teaspoon salt into a small cup. Add 1 tablespoon of olive oil, mix it up, and set it aside.

Prime and light your stove. Add two teaspoons of oil to your non-stick frying pan, and hold it over the flame to heat. When hot, add your first flattened dough piece. Cook it, moving the pan around so that your roughly 8" flatbread can cook evenly on your small burner. When the flatbread puckers with brown splotches on the underside, flip it over, and cook it on the other side until it, too, is blistered and blackened in spots. Transfer the flatbread back to its plate or cutting board and spread on half of the spice mixture.

Add another two teaspoons of oil to the frying pan, and proceed with your second flatbread as you did the first. When both sides are splotchy, blistered, and delicious-looking, remove it from the heat and spread on the remaining herbed topping. Devour it while it's still hot.

A tomato-mozzarella calzone is the tip of the iceberg—try any filling you want! See page 233 for ideas that will get your culinary creativity flowing.

*A hot, blistery calzone stuffed with cheese and warm tomatoes is yet another delicious variation of the simple tortilla dough recipe on page 222. You'll spread out your dough, fill it with goodies, and close it up. You'll fry it in a bit of oil until the outside crisps up and the inside gets melty, and you'll have yourself a feast of epic proportions. For best results, give yourself ample time and energy to tackle this recipe. Before you begin, be sure to review the "fun with dough" section on page 221, and the calzone-making photos on page 232.*

# tomato mozzarella calzone

*Prep & cook time: 30 minutes*
*Makes: 1 gigantic calzone*
*Difficulty: expert*

> 8 tablespoons (½ cup) flour
> ¼ teaspoon salt for the dough
> enough water to form a dough (about 4 tablespoons)
> 2oz / 57g firm mozzarella cheese
> 1 small tomato, or half a medium tomato
> a small wedge of onion (about 1 teaspoon, minced)
> 1 clove garlic
> pinch of salt for the filling
> ¼ teaspoon basil
> ¼ teaspoon oregano
> pinch of chili flakes
> a bit of water
> 1 tablespoon oil

First, make the dough: into your large non-stick cooking pot, measure the flour and salt, and combine them with your wooden spoon. Then, add water and stir until you're able to combine everything into a rough-looking ball of dough.

With floured fingers, squish it in your hands, turning and squashing until it becomes smoother, and of a more uniform consistency. The dough should not be overly sticky, so be sure to add a bit more flour if it is.

Place the dough on your large plate. Flatten it with your fingers, then take a can of beans (or a bottle of olive oil, or whatever you can find) to it, rolling until it is very thin, and slightly smaller than the size of your skillet. If you develop any tears or holes, don't worry. Just grab a bit of thick dough from somewhere else and smoosh it over the hole, using a bit of water as glue. After flattening your dough, let it sit while you clean up your working area and set up your cookset.

Next, prepare the rest of your ingredients: cut the mozzarella into thin slices. Arrange them on one half of your dough, leaving an empty space along the outside edge, as shown in the middle photo on page 232.

Chop the tomato into quarters, and discard the seeds and juice (the wet insides will create a soggy calzone). Then, chop the quarters into small chunks, and arrange them over the layer of cheese. Mince the garlic and onion into small pieces, and scatter them atop the tomatoes. Sprinkle on the basil, oregano, salt and chili flakes.

Dab the empty perimeter of the calzone with a touch of water (this will act as glue), and fold the empty half over the loaded half, gently stretching and easing it over the filling, creating a half-moon shape. Seal the edge by pressing it with the tines of your spork, or by pinching it closed with your fingers.

Now it's time to fry: measure one tablespoon of oil into your frying pan. Prime and light your stove, and turn it down to a low setting. Hold the pan over the flame to heat. The oil is hot enough when a droplet of water flicked into it sizzles. Carefully place your calzone into the oil. Fry it on one side, swirling the oil gently to help cook the doughy sides. The seam and the fold are the doughiest parts, so move the calzone around to make sure each area gets cooked.

When the calzone is speckled with brown on the underside, carefully flip it over with your spatula. Cook the second side, swirling as you did for the first, so that the oil cooks the doughiest parts. When the second side is lightly browned and cooked, transfer the calzone to a plate. Let cool slightly (don't burn your tongue on melted cheese), and enjoy!

# MORE DELICIOUS CALZONE FILLINGS:

**pepperoni pizza:** Start with a smear of marinara sauce (to make your own, see page 190) and top with minced onions, sliced pepperoni, mozzarella cheese, and chopped mushrooms. Sprinkle with salt, pepper, oregano, basil, and chili flakes.

**eggplant parmesan:** Sautée eggplant in olive oil, and mix with a spoonful or two of marinara sauce. Add the cooled filling to your dough, along with a generous amount of shaved parmesan and sliced mozzarella cheese. Salt and pepper to finish.

**pesto & tomatoes:** Spread a layer of pesto onto your dough, and top with tomato chunks and slices of mozzarella cheese. Season with salt, pepper, and chili flakes.

**cheesy spinach & garlic:** Sautée spinach in a bit of olive oil with a generous amount of minced garlic. Season with salt and pepper, and add the mostly-cooled mixture to your dough along with sliced mozzarella and crumbled feta cheeses.

**pot pie:** Let leftover pot pie stew (page 178) cool slightly, and use it as a calzone-stuffer.

Tyler cooking at sunset on the coast of Italy

# DESSERTS

Slicing apples to make apple turnovers in Russia

*This simple spiced applesauce is a comforting dish that can be served for dessert or even breakfast, depending on your mood. For added decadence, make the nutty, oat-filled topping on page 240 and enjoy a camp-friendly apple crumble, best served on a chilly autumn night in front of a crackling campfire.*

# spice-kissed applesauce

*Prep & cook time: 20 minutes*
*Makes: 2 servings*
*Difficulty: easy*

3 large apples
5 tablespoons water
1 tablespoon lemon juice (a generous squeeze)
3 tablespoons sugar
¾ teaspoon cinnamon
¼ teaspoon ground ginger
a generous pinch of cloves
a generous pinch of nutmeg
a pinch of salt

Cut the apples (peeled or not, depending on your preference) into small chunks, removing the cores and any bad spots as you go. Transfer the chunks to your large cooking pot. Add the rest of the ingredients, and give them a stir.

Prime and light your stove, and turn it to the lowest setting. Cook the apples, covered, lifting the lid occasionally to investigate: stir the apples around, and poke at them every now and then to test their softness. You want the apples to cook slowly without burning, so if the water is evaporating too quickly, add a little bit more.

When the apples are soft, smash them with the back of your wooden spoon until you're left with a chunky sauce. Some apples are more suited to this task than others—yours may disintegrate completely, or they may break down only if you use some force. Either way, the applesauce will be delicious.

Take the pot off the flame and turn off your stove. If you're making an apple crumble, set the fruit aside, covering it with a lid to keep warm, and move on to the nutty topping on page 240. Otherwise, enjoy!

*What's better than chunky, spiced applesauce (page 238)? How about a bowl of apple crumble, warm from the stove, with a crunchy, nutty, crumbly crust? If apples aren't your thing, why not try this addictive topping over a pan of caramelized bananas (page 248)?*

# crumble topping

*Prep & cook time: 15 minutes*
*Makes: 2 small servings*
*Difficulty: easy*

a small handful of walnuts, pecans, hazelnuts, or almonds (about 2 tablespoons chopped)
2 tablespoons butter
2 tablespoons flour
2 tablespoons sugar
3 tablespoons rolled oats
a pinch of salt
spice-kissed applesauce (page 238) or caramelized bananas (page 248) (optional)

Take a small handful of walnuts, pecans, hazelnuts, or almonds, and roughly chop them until you have about two tablespoons. (Crushing the nuts with the flat side of a knife works pretty well, too.) Add the nut pieces to your frying pan, and then add the rest of the ingredients.

Prime and light your cookstove, and set the frying pan onto a low flame. With your wooden spoon, stir the butter around so it melts quickly, then stir all of the ingredients together. Sauté until the mixture for about two minutes, or until it is lightly toasted. Turn off the heat and allow the crumble to cool slightly before serving it as a topping.

*These dumpling-like fried turnovers, oozing with melty chocolate and warm cherry jam, are worth the little bit of time and effort they require. Don't be daunted by the craft-project nature of this recipe—just make sure you are in good spirits and have time and water to spare when you're ready to tackle it (see "fun with dough" on page 221). Not a fan of chocolate and cherries together? You'll find more filling options on page 245.*

# cherry chocolate turnovers

*Prep & cook time: 30 minutes*
*Makes: 2 servings, or about 4 turnovers*
*Difficulty: expert*

8 tablespoons (½ cup) flour, plus more for sprinkling
½ teaspoon sugar
Large pinch of salt
enough water to form a dough (3-4 tablespoons)
2-3 tablespoons cherry jam (1-2 teaspoons per turnover)
1oz / 28g dark chocolate
1 tablespoon butter
sugar for sprinkling

First, get started with the dough: add the flour, sugar, and salt to your large cooking pot, and stir to combine with your wooden spoon. Now add the water, and mix until it forms a rough ball of dough. With floured fingers, squish the ball of dough, kneading it in your palm until it's smoother and of a more even consistency.

Tear the dough into four pieces, and squish them into ovals on a flat surface such as your cutting board or large plate.

Flour your hands and workspace as necessary so as not to get too sticky.

While you let the dough rounds rest, chop the chocolate into small pieces wherever you can find space on your cutting board. Get out your jam and your measuring spoons.

Now, it's time to assemble. Add one or two scant teaspoons of jam and a quarter of the chopped chocolate to one side of a dough oval, leaving a some empty space around the perimeter. Run a water-moistened finger along the border, and gently stretch the empty dough over the filling, creating a half-moon shape. Seal the edge by pressing it with the tines of your spork, or by folding it in on itself. Repeat with the other three turnovers.

When all of the turnovers are assembled and sealed, prime and light your stove. Add the butter to your frying pan, and heat it over a low flame until it's hot and melted. Fry all four turnovers at the same time, flipping them over when the first side is speckled and golden brown. Cook the second side until it's golden brown too, then transfer them to a plate and sprinkle with sugar before serving. Yum!

## MORE TASTY FILLINGS:

**chunky spiced apples:** Fill the dough with spoonfuls of cooled applesauce (page 238). Sprinkle finished turnovers with sugar and cinnamon.

**chocolate and banana:** Top the dough with a slice of banana and some chopped dark chocolate or chocolate chips.

**chocolate and peanut butter:** Fill the dough with a teaspoon or two of peanut butter, and a heap of chopped chocolate or chocolate chips.

**fresh cheese and honey:** Fill the dough with a spoonful of ricotta or mascarpone cheese, and a glob of local honey. Drizzle the finished turnovers with a bit more honey.

*I've always loved the way my grandmother prepares strawberries. She slices them, mixes them with sugar, and lets them sit on the counter until they release their syrupy red juice. I've adapted her time-tested method to the camp kitchen, resulting in this simple summery dessert.*

# strawberries in syrup

*Prep & wait time: 30 minutes*
*Makes: 2 small servings*
*Difficulty: easy*

1 pint (2 cups / 454g) ripe strawberries
3 tablespoons sugar

Using the tip of your knife, cut out the stems of the strawberries and discard them. Then, slice the berries into your large cooking pot and sprinkle them with sugar. Give them a stir with your wooden spoon so the sugar is evenly mixed in.

Cover the pot with its lid, and let it sit for about twenty or thirty minutes. During this time, check on the berries occasionally, giving them a stir and smooshing some of them lightly with the back of your spoon. When a half an hour has passed, or when the berries are positively swimming in their own crimson syrup, they're ready to eat.

These berries are delicious whether served over ice cream (perhaps there's a shop nearby?), or homemade treats like buttery crepes (page 123) and French toast (page 116). Alternatively, why not add vodka, white wine, or red wine, and drink the concoction as a fruity, camp-style cocktail?

*Butter and sugar transform a homely banana into a golden, caramelly delight! Should you wish to make more dessert than this recipe offers, make separate batches—you don't want to crowd the pan with too many banana slices, or they won't brown properly.*

# caramelized bananas

*Prep & cook time: 10 minutes*
*Makes: 1 serving*
*Difficulty: easy*

1 large, firm, ripe-but-not-mushy banana
1 tablespoon sugar
1 tablespoon butter

First, peel the banana. Cut it into three pieces, then slice each one in half, lengthwise. Place the six banana slices into your large cooking pot and sprinkle them with sugar. Rotate each slice with your fingers or a spoon, ensuring that sugar is coating each surface. Set aside.

Next, place the butter in your frying pan. Prime and light your cookstove, and turn it to a low setting. Melt the butter, then add the banana slices cut-side down. Fry until they're golden brown on the bottom (this takes a few minutes), then flip them over gently and fry them on the other side. When the bananas are golden brown all over, they're done.

Serve the bananas and their scrumptious sauce in buttery crepes (page 123), over ice cream (if you miraculously have some), or simply on their own.

*Lemon curd may sound fancy and complicated, but it's actually not too difficult to make, even on the road! Just be sure to follow the directions to a T, and have a look at the step-by-step photos on page 253. Armed with this recipe and a box of buttery shortbread cookies, you're in for one impressively luxurious treat! Why not stir it into yogurt, spoon it over cake, or wrap it in a buttery crepe (page 123)?*

# tangy lemon curd

*Prep, cook & wait time: 20 minutes*
*Makes: 2 servings*
*Difficulty: expert*

5 tablespoons sugar
3 tablespoons soft butter
1 egg
1 large lemon
water for boiling
shortbread or other buttery cookies (optional)

Measure the sugar and the soft butter into your frying pan and stir them together with a wooden spoon. Keep stirring until the mixture is fluffy and white. Crack an egg into the frying pan and mix it in thoroughly. Set aside.

Next, take your lemon and roll it on a hard surface (such as your cutting board), in order to get the juices flowing. Cut the lemon in half crosswise, and squeeze the juice into a small bowl. I do this by stabbing the cut side with a knife and rotating it as I squeeze the lemon. If you follow my method, be sure not to stab your palm in the process!

When you're done juicing, pick out the seeds and big chunks

of pith. Then, pour half of the juice into the egg mixture. Stir thoroughly, as shown in **Step 1** (opposite) and then add the rest of the juice, stirring until all of the juice is incorporated. At this point, it will look curdled and icky—don't worry, it will smooth out again as it cooks.

Now, on to the cooking. Because the lemon curd needs to be cooked over gentle heat, you're going to use your cooking pot as a makeshift double boiler. Fill your pot about a third of the way full of water. Set up your cookstove, and make sure it's level. Prime and light it, and turn it to low heat. Set the large pot of water (without a handle, if you only have one) onto the stove. When the water starts to get hot, set your frying pan on top, and hold its handle firmly. With your free hand, stir the mixture with your wooden spoon. Do so gently (you don't want it to slosh out of the pan), continuously (if you don't keep stirring, the curd will cook unevenly and become lumpy), and over the entire surface of the pan, including the edges and the center. The mixture will look like it does in the photo of **Step 2** (opposite).

As the curd begins to cook, the butter clumps will slowly melt. After that, you'll see a thin foam of tiny bubbles coating the surface, as shown in **Step 3** (opposite). Eventually, the foam will dissipate, and the curd will no longer be transparent. Instead, you'll have a glossy, creamy curd that can coat the back of your wooden spoon like a thin layer of pudding, as shown in the photo on page 250. At this point, it's done, so you can take it off the heat and allow it to cool.

Enjoy the lemon curd with shortbread, gingersnaps, or graham crackers. Or, use it as a topping for homemade crepes (page 123) or French toast (page 116). If there's some leftover, why not stir some into your morning yogurt?

*I've made variations of this rice pudding many times, and the recipe below is my favorite. With its rich creaminess and irresistible hints of honey, almond, and coconut, this dish makes for a deliciously satisfying dessert or hearty breakfast.*

# honey, almond, and coconut rice pudding

*Prep & cook time: 30 minutes*
*Makes: 2 servings*
*Difficulty: easy*

8 tablespoons (½ cup) rice
1 14oz / 400 ml can of coconut milk
¼ teaspoon salt
4 tablespoons honey
half a coconut milk can of water (a scant cup, 200 ml)
½ teaspoon lemon juice (a small squeeze)
¼ teaspoon almond extract
3 tablespoons almonds

Measure the rice, coconut milk, salt, and honey into your large cooking pot. Fill the empty coconut milk can half-full of water and add that, too. Prime and light your stove. Over a medium-high heat, boil the rice uncovered, stirring often, for 20-25 minutes. If the rice isn't tender by the time the liquid has evaporated, add a bit more water and keep cooking.

When the rice is soft, creamy, and has mostly absorbed the cooking liquid, remove it from the heat. Stir in the lemon juice and almond extract. Chop the almonds roughly (or leave them whole) and sprinkle them on top.

*The next time you're cozied up at camp for the night and a mad craving for chocolate overtakes you, reach into your well-stocked pedal-powered pantry and grab the ingredients to make these cookies. These basic mix-and-drop chocolate oat clusters may not be mom's warm chocolate chip cookies straight from the oven, but hey, they're the next best thing. In very hot weather, the cookies won't be as firm and sturdy as they are in cooler weather, but they still hit the spot.*

# chocolate fudge oat cookies

*Prep, cook & wait time: 20-45 minutes*
*Makes: 2 servings; 10-12 small cookies*
*Difficulty: easy*

3 oz / 85g semi-sweet chocolate
10 tablespoons oats
2 tablespoons sugar
1 tablespoon water
2 tablespoons butter
2 tablespoons peanut butter
a pinch of salt
¼ teaspoon almond extract or ½ teaspoon vanilla
cocoa (optional)
espresso powder (optional)
cinnamon (optional)
cayenne pepper (optional)

First, get your ingredients prepared: chop the chocolate into small chunks and place them in a small bowl along with the oats. Set the bowl aside. Next, measure the sugar, water, butter, peanut butter and salt into your large cooking pot.

Now, get cooking: prime and light your stove, and set the

cooking pot over low heat. Stir the mixture until the butter has melted and is bubbling all over. Immediately remove the pot from the stove, and dump in the oats and chocolate. Stir until all of the chocolate is melted, completely coating the oats. Mix in the almond or vanilla extract.

Spoon the chocolatey oats by the tablespoonful onto a large plate and/or cutting board, and allow the cookies to cool and harden for about a half an hour before eating. The less you poke and prod at them while they're cooling, the better they'll hold together.

After about a half an hour (depending on the humidity and temperature of your area) the cookies should be dry on the outside, sturdy enough to handle, and fudgy on the inside.

If you wish to experiment with various toppings: try them dusted with cocoa, espresso powder, or even cinnamon with the tiniest pinch of cayenne pepper.

*Mixing up a batch of chocolate fudge oat cookies (page 256)*

*Exploring a market in Bangkok, Thailand*

# INDEX

acidity
- balancing flavors . . . . . . . 36, 40, 92
- lemon(s) (see lemons)
- lime(s) (see limes)
- Vinaigrette dressing . . . . . . . . 151
- vinegar. . . . . . . . . . 40, 92, 147, 151

afternoon snacks . . . . . . . . . . . 63, 155

alcohol
- cocktail . . . . . . . . . . . . . . . . . . 247
- in cooking . . . . . . . . . . . . . . 92, 119

almond(s)
- Fruit and nut granola bar bites 156
- Honey, almond, and coconut rice pudding . . . . . . . . . . . . . . . . . . . 254
- in salad . . . . . . . . . . . . . . . . . . 152

almond extract
- about. . . . . . . . . . . . . . . . . . . 47, 52
- Chocolate fudge oat cookies . 256
- Honey, almond, and coconut rice pudding . . . . . . . . . . . . . . . . . . . 254

aluminum foil . . . . . . . . . . . . . . . . . 62

apple(s)
- Apple crumble . . . . . . . . . . . . 240
- cider vinegar . . . . . . . . . . . . 40, 151
- in grilled cheese . . . . . . . . . . . 182
- in salad . . . . . . . . . . . . . . . . . . 152
- Spice-kissed applesauce . . . . . 238

arugula . . . . . . . . . . . . . . . . . . . . . 151

Asian-inspired recipes
- Rice noodles with stir-fried broccoli and onions . . . . . 189-191
- Sweet-spicy peanut noodles. . 197
- Soy peanut cabbage slaw . . . . 142

avocado(s)
- Guacamole . . . . . . . . . . . . . . . 134
- in salads. . . . . . . . . . . . . . . . . . 152
- Mango and avocado salad . . . . 138
- preparation . . . . . . . . . . . . . . 76-77

bacon . . . . . . . . . . . . . . . . . . . 199, 206

bag(s) (see also pannier)
- for food storage . . . . . . . . . . . . 62
- spice bag . . . . . . . . . . . . . 44, 46-53

balsamic vinegar . . . . . . . . . . . . 40, 151

banana(s)
- Banana nut oatmeal . . . . . . . . 114
- Caramelized bananas . . . . . . . 248
- turnover filling . . . . . . . . . . . . 245

basic tools (see tools)

basil
- about. . . . . . . . . . . . . . . . . . . . . 49
- pesto . . . . . . . . . . . . . . 39, 182, 233

basin, waterproof . . . . 32, 79, 142, 152

bean(s) (see also green beans)
- Black bean summer salad . . . . 148
- canned. . . . . . . . . . . . . . . . . 38, 63
- Chili con carne . . . . . . . . . . . . 164
- Garlicky green beans . . . . . . . 218
- Lemony garlic bean spread . . . 135

beef . . . . . . . . . . . . . . . . . . . . . . . 164
Berlin-style *currywurst* . . . . . . . . . 205
Black bean summer salad . . . . . . . 148
black pepper . . . . . . . . . . . . . . . . . . 52
bouillon
    about . . . . . . . . . 47, 49, 92, 97, 180
    in recipes . . 167, 169, 174, 178, 210
bowl
    Ortlieb folding . . . . . . . . . . . . . 32
    Sea to Summit X-bowl . . . . . . . 28
    storage . . . . . . . . . . . . . . . . . . . 63
bratwurst
    Berlin-style *currywurst* . . . . . . . 205
bread
    about . . . . . . . . . . . . . . . . . . . . . 43
    Camp-style croutons . . . . 150-153
    French toast . . . . . . . . . . . . . . 116
    grilled cheese . . . . . . . . . . . . . 183
    Italian bread salad (*panzanella*) 146
    One-eyed-sailor . . . . . . . . . . . 106
    Rosemary flatbread with garlic and chili flakes . . . . . . . . . . . . . . . . 226
    sandwich ideas . . . . . . . . . . . . 144
    Tyler's tortillas . . . . . . . . . . . . 222
breakfast
    recipes . . . . . . . . . . . . . . . 100-125
    second breakfast . . . . . . . . 126-127
    Spicy scrambled egg burrito . . 108
broccoli
    preparing . . . . . . . . . . . . . . . . . 78
    Rice noodles with stir-fried broccoli and onion . . . . . . 189-191
Browned butter crepes . . . . . 123-125
bungee net . . . . . . . . . . . . . . . . . . 60
burrito . . . . . . . . . . . . . . . . . . . . . 108

butter
    about . . . . . . . . . . . . . . . . . . . 43, 97
    Browned butter crepes . . 123-125
    Caramelized bananas . . . . . . . 248
    cooking with . . . . . . . . . . . . . . 92
    in sauces . . . . . . . . . . . . . . . . . 212
    peanut (*see* peanut butter)
    storage . . . . . . . . . . . . . . . . . . 43
cabbage
    preparation . . . . . . . . . . . . . . . 78
    Soy peanut cabbage slaw . . . . 142
calzone
    fillings . . . . . . . . . . . . . . . . . . . 233
    Tomato mozzarella calzone . . 229
camp stove (*see* stove)
Camp-style croutons . . . . . . . . . . 153
Camper's tuna casserole . . . . . . . 202
can opener . . . . . . . . . . . . . . . . 29, 63
canned food
    beans (*see* beans)
    mystery can . . . . . . . . . . . . . 56-57
    staple ingredients . . . . . . . . 34-45
    storage . . . . . . . . . . . . . . . . . . 63
    why use canned food . . . . . 97-98
Caramelized bananas . . . . . . . . . . 248
carrot(s)
    as snacks . . . . . . . . . . . . . . . . 155
    in salad . . . . . . . . . . . . . . . . . 152
    Potato, carrot, and pea curry . 169
cayenne pepper . . . . . . . . 49, 205, 256
cereal
    Cinnamon raisin granola . . . . . 103
    for second breakfast . . . . . . . . 126

cheddar
- Camper's tuna casserole. . . . . 202
- over fried potatoes. . . . . . . . . 208
- Tyler's Grilled Cheese Sandwich . . . . . . . . . . . . . . . . . . . . . . . 183

Cheese (see also specific cheeses)
- about. . . . . . . . . . . . . . . . . . . . . 43
- calzone fillings. . . . . . . . . . . . . 233
- Camper's tuna casserole. . . . . 202
- Cheesy garlic pasta. . . . . . 186-188
- grilled cheese sandwich . . . . . 183
- Hearty meat and potatoes for a cold winter's night . . . . . . . . . 206
- in salad . . . . . . . . . . . . . . . . . . 152
- measuring . . . . . . . . . . . . . . . . 78
- on sandwiches. . . . . . . . . . . . . 144
- Pasta in creamy choose-your-own-cheese sauce. . . . . . . . . . . . . . 199
- snacks . . . . . . . . . . . . . . . . . . . 155
- storage . . . . . . . . . . . . . . . . . . 43
- Tomato mozzarella calzone . . 229
- turnover filling . . . . . . . . . . . . 245
- Tyler's grilled cheese sandwich. . . . . . . . . . . . . . . . . . . . . . . . . 183
- Zucchini feta fritters. . . . . . . . 214

Cherry chocolate turnovers . . . . 242

chili
- Chili con carne . . . . . . . . . . . . 164
- flakes. . . . . . . . . . . . . . . . . .49, 226
- Garlic-chili-herb fried eggs. . . 113
- powder . . . . . . . . . . . . . . . .49-50
- Rosemary flatbread with garlic and chili flakes . . . . . . . . . . . . .49, 226

chips. . . . . . . . . . . . . . . . . . . .155, 202

chocolate
- about. . . . . . . . . . . . . . . . . . . . . 44
- Cherry chocolate turnovers . 242
- Chocolate fudge oat cookies . 256
- snacks . . . . . . . . . . . . . . . . . . . 155
- turnover fillings. . . . . . . . . . . . 245

cilantro
- Black bean summer salad . . . . 148
- Fresh tomato salsa . . . . . . . . . 133

cinnamon
- about. . . . . . . . . . . . . . . . . . . . . 50
- Cinnamon raisin granola. . . . . 103
- Spice-kissed applesauce . . . . . 238
- Tomato soup. . . . . . . . . . . . . . 176

Cinnamon raisin granola . . . . . . . 103

citrus (see lemon or lime)

cleaning (see dishwashing)

cloves . . . . . . . . . . . . . . . .51, 176, 238

cocktail. . . . . . . . . . . . . . . . . . . . . 247

coconut
- milk . . . . . . . . . . . . . . . . . . . . . . 41
- Honey, almond and coconut rice pudding . . . . . . . . . . . . . . . . . 254
- Potato, carrot, and pea curry . 169
- shredded. . . . . . . . . . . . . . . . . 156

containers (see also individual items to be stored)
- about. . . . . . . . . . . . . 32, 36, 38, 43
- packing panniers . . . . . . . . . .60-64

cook stove (see stove)

cookies
- as snacks . . . . . . . . . . . . . . .44, 155
- Chocolate fudge oat cookies . 256

INDEX 263

cooking
  creatively (see winging it)
  pannier . . . . . . . . . . . . . . . . . 63-64
  tips . . . . . . . . . . . . . . . . . . . . 70-83
  utensils . . . . . . . . . . . . . . . . . . . 28
cookset
  about. . . . . . . . . . . . . . . . . . . . 24, 70
  cooking with . . . . . . . . 99, 123, 186
  importance of non-stick. . 70, 87, 99
  storage . . . . . . . . . . . . . . . . . . . 63
  washing . . . . . . . . . . . . . . . . . . 87
corn
  Black bean summer salad . . . . 148
crackers . . . . . . . . . . . . . . . . . . . . . 155
cranberries, dried
  as snacks . . . . . . . . . . . . . . . . . . 40
  Fruit and nut granola gar bites 156
  in salads. . . . . . . . . . . . . . . . . . 152
Creamy choose-your-own cheese
sauce. . . . . . . . . . . . . . . . . . . . . . . 199
Creamy potato leek soup . . . . . . 167
creative cooking (see winging it)
croutons. . . . . . . . . . . . . . . . . . . . 153
Crepes, browned butter . . . . 123-125
Crumble topping . . . . . . . . . . . . . 240
cucumber
  in mixed salad . . . . . . . . . . . . . 152
  Tunisian tomato and cucumber
  salad (salade tunisienne). . . . . . 147
cumin . . . . . . . . . . . . . . . . . . . . . . . 50
Curd, tangy lemon . . . . . . . . . . . . 251
curry
  Berlin-style currywurst. . . . . . . . 205
  paste . . . . . . . . . . . . . . . . . . . . . 45
  Potato, carrot and pea curry . 169

curry (continued)
  powder . . . . . . . . . . . . 50, 169, 205
cutting board . . . . . . . . . . . . 28, 29, 64
dairy (see specific dairy products)
dressing . . . . . . . . . . . . . . . . . 151-152
dessert recipes. . . . . . . . . . . . 236-259
dinner recipes. . . . . . . . . . . . . 162-235
dip
  Guacamole . . . . . . . . . . . . . . . 134
  Lemony garlic bean spread. . . 135
dishes
  choosing . . . . . . . . . . . . . . . . . . 28
  storage . . . . . . . . . . . . . . . . . . . 63
dishwashing . . . . . . . . . . . . 32, 86, 87
double boiler . . . . . . . . . . . . . . 90, 251
dough
  Cherry chocolate turnovers . 242
  dough-making tips. . . . . . . . . . 221
  Rosemary flatbread with garlic and
  chili flakes . . . . . . . . . . . . . . . 226
  Tomato mozzarella calzone . . 229
  Tyler's tortillas . . . . . . . . . . . . 222
dressing, Vinaigrette . . . . . . . . . . . 151
dried fruit
  about. . . . . . . . . . . . . . . . . . . . . 41
  as snacks . . . . . . . . . . . . . . . . . 155
  Cinnamon raisin granola. . . . . 103
  Fruit and nut granola bar bites 156
  in salad . . . . . . . . . . . . . . . . . . 152
dumplings
  Cherry chocolate turnovers . 242
  Tyler's dumplings. . . . . . . . 174-175
emergency rations . . . . . . . . . . . . . 44
egg(s)
  about. . . . . . . . . . . . . . . 41, 104-105

egg(s) (*continued*)

    Browned butter crepes . . 123-125

    French toast . . . . . . . . . . . . . . 116

    Garlic-chili-herb fried eggs . . . 113

    Hard-boiled eggs . . . . 144, 152, 159

    One-eyed-sailor . . . . . . . . . . . 106

    Spicy scrambled egg breakfast burrito . . . . . . . . . . . 108

Egg-in-a-basket . . . . . . . . . . . . . . . 106

eggplant

    calzone filling . . . . . . . . . . . . . 233

    collecting free . . . . . . . . . . . . . 59

evaporated milk

    about . . . . . . . . . . . . . . . . . . . . 41

    Camper's tuna casserole . . . . . 202

    Creamy potato leek soup . . . . 167

    Pasta in creamy choose-your-own cheese sauce . . . . . . . . . . . . . . 199

extracts (see almond / vanilla extract)

feta cheese

    Zucchini and Feta Fritters . . . 214

filtration (see water)

fire-starting . . . . . . . . . . . 28, 63, 71, 73

fish

    Camper's tuna casserole . . . . . 202

    canned . . . . . . . . . . 45, 56, 144, 147

flatbread

    Rosemary flatbread with garlic and chili flakes . . . . . . . . . . . . . . . . 226

    Tyler's tortillas . . . . . . . . . . . . 222

flint & steel (see fire-starting)

flour

    dough-making (see also dough) 221

    in roux . . . . . . . . . . . . . . . . . . 212

    purchasing . . . . . . . . . . . . . . . . 35

flour (*continued*)

    Rosemary flatbread with garlic and chili flakes . . . . . . . . . . . . . . . . 226

    storing . . . . . . . . . . . . . . . . . . . 35

    Tomato mozzarella calzone . . 229

    Tyler's tortillas . . . . . . . . . . . . 222

foil, aluminum . . . . . . . . . . . . . . . . . 62

food safety . . . . . . . . . . . . . . 34, 39, 40

food storage . . . . . 35, 36, 38, 43, 60-65

foraging . . . . . . . . . . . . . . . . . . . . . . 59

Fudge, chocolate oat cookies . . . . 256

fuel bottle

    about . . . . . . . . . . . . . . . . 25, 73, 74

    filling . . . . . . . . . . . . . . . . . . . . 26

    storing . . . . . . . . . . . . . . . . . . . 64

French toast . . . . . . . . . . . . . . . . . 116

Fresh tomato salsa . . . . . . . . . . . . 133

Fritters, zucchini feta . . . . . . . . . . 214

fruit (see *also specific fruits*)

    as snacks . . . . . . . . . . . . . . 126, 155

    Caramelized bananas . . . . . . . 248

    Cherry chocolate turnovers . 242

    dried (see *dried fruit*)

    Fruit and nut granola bar bites 156

    in salad . . . . . . . . . . . . . . . . . . 152

    Mango and avocado aalad . . . . 138

    Plum and peach jam . . . . . . . . 118

    Spice-kissed applesauce . . . . . 138

    Strawberries in syrup . . . . . . . 247

Fruit and nut granola bar bites . . 156

frying

    Cherry chocolate turnovers . 242

    Fried potatoes . . . . . . . . . 206-209

    Rosemary flatbread with garlic and chili flakes . . . . . . . . . . . . . . . . 226

frying (*continued*)
    tips . . . . . . . . . . . . . . . . . . . . 216-217
    Tomato mozzarella calzone . . 229
    Zucchini feta fritters. . . . . . . . 214

garlic
    fresh . . . . . . . . . . . . . . . . . . . . 39, 50
    Garlic-chili-herb fried eggs . . . 113
    Garlicky green beans . . . . . . . 218
    granules or powdered . . . . . . . 51
    Lemony garlic bean spread. . . 135
    Our very favorite cheesy garlic pasta . . . . . . . . . . . . . . . . . 186-188
    preparing. . . . . . . . . . . . . . . . 78-79
    Rosemary flatbread with garlic and chili flakes . . . . . . . . . . . . . . . . 226
    Tyler's grilled cheese. . . . . . . . 183

Ginger
    about. . . . . . . . . . . . . . . . . . . . . . 51
    Potato, carrot, and pea curry . 169
    Rice noodles with stir-fried broccoli and onion . . . . . . 189-191
    Soy peanut cabbage slaw . . . . 142
    Spice-kissed applesauce . . . . . 238

gleaning (see foraging)

gnocci (see pasta)

gouda, smoked
    Meat and potatoes for a cold winter's night . . . . . . . . . . . . . 206

granola
    Cinnamon raisin granola. . . . . 103
    Fruit and nut granola bar bites 156

grater . . . . . . . . . . . . . . . . . . . . . . . 90

gravy
    making, step-by-step . . . . . . . . 212

gravy (*continued*)
    Smashed potatoes and gravy . 210

greens
    Mixed salad with vinaigrette dressing. . . . . . . . . . . . . . . . . . 151

green beans
    Garlicky green beans . . . . . . . 218
    Hearty pot pie stew . . . . . . . . 178

grilled cheese . . . . . . . . . . . . . . . . 183

groceries
    organizing . . . . . . . . . . . . . . 62-65
    packing . . . . . . . . . . . . . . . . 60-62
    shopping . . . . . . . . . . . . . . 55-56

GSI Pinnacle Backpacker Cookset. 24

Guacamole . . . . . . . . . . . . . . . . . . 134

handlebar bag . . . . . . . . . . . . . . . . 64

Hard-boiled eggs . . . . . . . . . . . . . 159
    in salad . . . . . . . . . . . . . . . . . . 152
    on *Salade tunisienne*. . . . . . . . 147
    on sandwiches. . . . . . . . . . . . . 144

Hearty meat and potatoes for a cold winter's night . . . . . . . . . . . . . . . . 206

Hearty pot pie stew. . . . . . . . . . . 178

herb(s)
    cooking with . . . . . . . . . . . . . 88, 92
    Garlic-chili-herb fried egg. . . . 113
    Rosemary flatbread with garlic and chili flakes . . . . . . . . . . . . . . . . 226
    spice bag . . . . . . . . . . . . . 44, 46-53

Home soup with Tyler's dumplings . . . . . . . . . . . . . . . . . . . . . . . . . . . 173-175

honey
    about. . . . . . . . . . . . . . . . . . . . . 43
    and cheese turnover filling . . . 245

honey (*continued*)
- Fruit and nut granola bar bites 156
- Honey, almond, and coconut rice pudding . . . . . . . . . . . . . . . . . . 254

ingredients
- about . . . . . . . . . . . . . . . . . 91, 97, 98
- preparing . . . . . . . . . 74, 76-83, 140
- staple . . . . . . . . . . . . . . . . . . . . 34-44

iodine (*see* water purification)

Italian bread salad (*panzanella*) . . 146

Jalapeño pepper
- Black bean summer salad . . . . 148
- Fresh tomato salsa . . . . . . . . . 133
- Mango and avocado salad . . . . 138
- preparing . . . . . . . . . . . . . . . . . . 79

jam
- about . . . . . . . . . . . . . . . . . . . . . . 41
- Cherry chocolate turnovers . 242
- jam-making advice . . . . . . . 119-121
- on grilled cheese . . . . . . . . . . . 182
- Plum & peach jam . . . . . . . . . . 118

ketchup
- about . . . . . . . . . . . . . . . . . . . . . . 39
- Berlin-style *currywurst* . . . . . . . 205
- on fried potatoes . . . . . . . . . . 208

kidney beans . . . . . . . . . . . . . . . . . 164

knives . . . . . . . . . . . . . . . . . . . . . 28, 64

ladle . . . . . . . . . . . . . . . . . . . . . . . . 28

leek(s)
- Potato leek soup . . . . . . . . . . . 167
- preparing . . . . . . . . . . . . . . . . . . 79

lemon(s) (*see also* acidity)
- about . . . . . . . . . . . . . . . . . . . . . . 40
- curd . . . . . . . . . . . . . . . . . . . . . 251

lemon(s) (*continued*)
- for hard-boiling eggs . . . . . . . . 159
- juicing . . . . . . . . . . . . . . . . . . . . 80
- Lemony garlic bean spread . . . 135
- Tangy lemon curd . . . . . . . . . . 251

Lemony garlic bean spread . . . . . 135

lettuce
- on sandwiches . . . . . . . . . . . . . 144
- Salad with vinaigrette dressing 151
- washing . . . . . . . . . . . . . . . . . . 150

lighter (*see* fire-starting)

lime(s) (*see also* acidity)
- about . . . . . . . . . . . . . . . . . . . . . . 40
- Black bean summer salad . . . . 148
- Fresh tomato salsa . . . . . . . . . 133
- Potato, carrot, and pea curry . 169
- Sweet-spicy peanut noodles . . 197

lunch recipes . . . . . . . . . . . . . 130-161

mango
- Mango and avocado salad . . . . 138
- preparing . . . . . . . . . . . . . . 140-141

Marinara sauce . . . . . . . . . . . . . . . 194

Mashed potatoes and gravy . . . . . 210

measuring . . . . . . . . . . . . . . . . . . . . 29

measuring spoons . . . . . . . . . . . . . 29

meat
- Berlin-style *currywurst* . . . . . . . 205
- Chili con carne . . . . . . . . . . . . 164
- Hearty meat and potatoes for a cold winter's night . . . . . . . . . 206
- in salads . . . . . . . . . . . . . . . . . . 151
- on sandwiches . . . . . . . . . . . . . 144
- shopping . . . . . . . . . . . . . . . . . . 55

milk
- about . . . . . . . . . . . . . . . . . . . . . 41
- cereal . . . . . . . . . . . . . . . . . . . . 126
- coconut (see coconut milk)
- evaporated (see evaporated milk)
- ultra-heat treated (UHT) . . . . . 41

Mixed salad with vinaigrette dressing . . . . . . . . . . . . . . . . . . . . . . . . . . 151

mozzarella
- Our very favorite cheesy garlic pasta . . . . . . . . . . . . . . . . . . . . 186
- Tomato mozzarella calzone . . 229
- Tyler's grilled cheese sandwich 183

MSR
- Alpine spoon . . . . . . . . . . . . . . 28
- fuel bottle . . . . . . . . . . . . . . . . 25
- Whisperlite . . . . . . . . . . 25, 73, 96

mug . . . . . . . . . . . . . . . . . . . . . . . . 28

mustard
- Vinaigrette dressing . . . . . . . . 151

non-stick cookset
- about . . . . . . . . . . . . . . . . . . 24, 70
- cooking with . . . . . . . 99, 123, 186
- importance of non-stick . . 70, 87, 99
- storage . . . . . . . . . . . . . . . . . . . 63
- washing . . . . . . . . . . . . . . . . . . 87

noodles (see pasta)

nut(s) (see also specific nuts)
- as snacks . . . . . . . . . . . . . . . . 155
- Banana nut oatmeal . . . . . . . . 114
- Crumble topping . . . . . . . . . . . 240
- Fruit and nut granola bar bites 156
- Honey, almond, and coconut rice pudding . . . . . . . . . . . . . . . . . 254

nut(s) (continued)
- in salad . . . . . . . . . . . . . . . . . 152
- Soy peanut cabbage slaw . . . . 142
- Sweet-spicy peanut noodles . . 197

Nutella . . . . . . . . . . . . . . . . . . . . . 125

nutmeg . . . . . . . . . . . . . . . 51, 176, 238

oats
- about . . . . . . . . . . . . . . . . . . . . 38
- Banana nut oatmeal . . . . . . . . 114
- Chocolate fudge oat cookies . 256
- Cinnamon raisin granola . . . . . 103
- Crumble topping . . . . . . . . . . . 240
- Fruit and nut granola bar bites 156

oil
- about . . . . . . . . . . . . . . . . . . . . 39
- frying with . . . . . . . . . . . . . . . 216
- storage . . . . . . . . . . . . . . . . . . . 63
- Vinaigrette dressing . . . . . . . . 151

olive(s)
- oil (see oil)
- on *Salade Tunisienne* . . . . . . . . 147

One-eyed sailor . . . . . . . . . . . . . . 106

onion(s)
- about . . . . . . . . . . . . . . . . . . . . 38
- in salad . . . . . . . . . . . . . . . . . 152
- powdered . . . . . . . . . . . . . . . . 51
- preparing . . . . . . . . . . . . . . . . . 80
- Rice noodles with stir-fried broccoli and onion . . . . . . 189-191
- storage . . . . . . . . . . . . . . . . 38, 63

orange(s)
- as snacks . . . . . . . . . . . . . . . . 155
- in salad . . . . . . . . . . . . . . . . . 152

oregano . . . . . . . . . . . . . . . . . . . . . 51

organizing . . . . . . . . . . . . . . . . . . 62-65
Ortlieb
    folding bowl . . . . . . . . . . . . . . . 32
    panniers. . . . . . . . . . . . . . . . . 62-63
Our very favorite cheesy garlic pasta
. . . . . . . . . . . . . . . . . . . . . . . 186-188
packing . . . . . . . . . . . . . . . . . . . 60-65
pad thai. . . . . . . . . . . . . . . . . . . . . 197
pannier(s)
    cooking . . . . . . . . . . . . . . . . . 63-64
    explosion. . . . . . . . . . . . . . . . 66-67
    organization . . . . . . . . . . . . . 62-65
    packing . . . . . . . . . . . . . . . . . 60, 62
    pantry . . . . . . . . . . . . . . . . . . . . . 63
    snack . . . . . . . . . . . . . . . . . . . . . 63
    weight distribution . . . . . . . . . . 65
pantry
    pannier . . . . . . . . . . . . . . . . . . . 63
    staples . . . . . . . . . . . . . . . . . . 34-45
panzanella (Italian bread salad) . . 146
paprika . . . . . . . . . . . . . . . . . . 51, 205
parmesan (see also cheese)
    about. . . . . . . . . . . . . . . . . . . . . 43
    calzone filling, eggplant . . . . . . 233
    on spaghetti marinara. . . . . . . . 194
    Our very favorite cheesy garlic
    pasta . . . . . . . . . . . . . . . . . . . 186
    Pasta in creamy, choose-your-own
    cheese sauce. . . . . . . . . . . . . . 199
pasta
    about. . . . . . . . . . . . . . . . . . . . . 36
    cooking tips. . . . . . . . . . . . . 36, 185
    Camper's tuna casserole. . . . . 202
    gnocci . . . . . . . . . . . . . . . . . . . . 36

pasta (continued)
    Our very favorite cheesy garlic
    pasta . . . . . . . . . . . . . . . . . 186-188
    Pasta in creamy, choose-your-own-
    cheese sauce. . . . . . . . . . . . . . 199
    ramen . . . . . . . . . . . . . . . . . . . . 44
    Rice noodles with stir-fried
    broccoli and onion . . . . . . 189-191
    Spaghetti marinara . . . . . . . . . 194
    storage . . . . . . . . . . . . . . . . . . . 36
    Sweet-spicy peanut noodles. . 197
pastries
    Cherry chocolate turnovers . 242
    for second breakfast. . . . . . . . 126
pea(s)
    Camper's tuna casserole. . . . . 202
    Potato, carrot, and pea curry . 169
    sugar-snaps in salads . . . . . . . . 152
Peach and plum jam . . . . . . . . . . . 118
peanut(s)
    as snacks . . . . . . . . . . . . . . . . . 41
    Soy peanut cabbage slaw . . . . 142
    Sweet spicy peanut noodles. . 197
peanut butter
    about. . . . . . . . . . . . . . . . . . . . . 40
    and chocolate turnover filling. 245
    Banana nut oatmeal . . . . . . . . 114
    Chocolate fudge oat cookies . 256
    Fruit and nut granola bar bites 156
    Sweet-Spicy Peanut Noodles . 197
pear(s)
    on grilled cheese sandwich. . . 182
    on salad . . . . . . . . . . . . . . . . . 152
peeler, vegetable. . . . . . . . . . . . 29, 63

pepper, bell
- Black bean summer salad . . . . 148
- in salad . . . . . . . . . . . . . . . . . 152

pepper, black. . . . . . . . . . . . . . . . . 52

pepper, cayenne . . . . . . . . 49, 205, 256

pepper, chili. . . . . . . . . . . . . . .49, 226

pepper, jalapeño (see jalapeño pepper)

pepperoni pizza calzone. . . . . . . . 233

pesto
- about. . . . . . . . . . . . . . . . . . . . 39
- calzone fillings. . . . . . . . . . . . . 233
- in grilled cheese sandwiches. . 182

pie, pot . . . . . . . . . . . . . . . . . . . . 178

pizza, pepperoni . . . . . . . . . . . . . 233

plate . . . . . . . . . . . . . . . . . . . . .28, 64

Plum and Peach Jam . . . . . . . . . . . 118

pocket knife (see knives)

porridge (see oats)

Pot Pie Stew. . . . . . . . . . . . . . . . . 178
- calzone filling. . . . . . . . . . . . . 233

potato(es)
- about. . . . . . . . . . . . . . . . . . . . 36
- Creamy potato leek soup. . . . 167
- Hearty pot pie stew . . . . . . . . 178
- how to prepare. . . . . . . . . . .80-81
- Meat and potatoes for a cold winter's night . . . . . . . . . . . . . 206
- Potato, carrot, and pea curry . 169
- Smashed potatoes and gravy . 210
- storage . . . . . . . . . . . . . . . .36, 63
- Tyler's fried potatoes . . . . . . . 208

preparing ingredients . . . . . 76-83, 140

pudding
- Honey, almond, and coconut rice pudding . . . . . . . . . . . . . . . . . 254

radish(es) . . . . . . . . . . . . . . . . . . 152

raisin(s)
- as snacks . . . . . . . . . . . . . . . . . 40
- Cinnamon raisin granola. . . . . 103
- Fruit and nut granola bar bites 156
- in salad . . . . . . . . . . . . . . . . . 152

ramen noodles . . . . . . . . . . . . . . . 44

recycling . . . . . . . . . . . . . . . . . . . . 60

re-potting . . . . . . . . . . . . . . . . . . . 60

rice
- about. . . . . . . . . . . . . . . . . . . . 38
- Honey, almond, and coconut rice pudding . . . . . . . . . . . . . . . . . 254
- Rice noodles in peanut sauce . 197
- Rice noodles with stir-fried brocolli and onion. . . . . . . 189-191

rosemary
- about. . . . . . . . . . . . . . . . . . . . 52
- Rosemary flatbread with garlic and chili flakes . . . . . . . . . . . . . . . 226

roux . . . . . . . . . . . . . . . . . . .212-213

salad(s)
- Black bean summer salad . . . . 148
- Mango and avocado salad. . . . 138
- Mixed salad with vinaigrette dressing. . . . . . . . . . . . . . . . . 151
- *panzanella* (Italian bread salad) 146
- *Salade Tunisienne* (Tunisian tomato and cucumber salad). . . . . . . . 147
- Soy peanut cabbage slaw . . . . 142

*Salade Tunisienne* . . . . . . . . . . . . . 147

salsa .................... 133

salt

    about.................... 35

    in pasta water............. 185

    storage .................. 63

sandwich(es)

    ideas .................... 144

    Tyler's grilled cheese......... 183

sauce(s)

    applesauce................ 238

    basic cheese .............. 199

    gravy ................210-213

    marinara ................. 194

    soy (see soy sauce)

    vinaigrette................ 151

sausage(s)

    Berlin-style *currywurst*....... 205

Scrambled egg breakfast burrito . 108

screen (see wind screen)

Sea to Summit dishes........... 28

seasoning ..................91-92

second breakfast ..........126-127

Serbian salad................. 147

shopping...................55-56

slaw, Soy peanut cabbage ....... 142

Smashed potatoes and gravy .... 210

snack(s)

    afternoon ................ 155

    importance of...........70-71

    pannier .................. 63

Snow Peak titanium spork....... 29

soap ...................32, 63, 87

soup(s)

    Chili con carne ............ 164

soup(s) (*continued*)

    cooking without a recipe . 180-181

    Creamy potato leek soup.... 167

    Home soup............... 174

    Pot pie stew .............. 178

    Potato, carrot, and pea curry . 169

    Tomato soup.............. 176

soy sauce

    about.................... 40

    Rice noodles with stir-fried broccoli and onion ......189-191

    Soy peanut cabbage slaw .... 142

    Sweet-spicy peanut noodles.. 197

spaghetti (*see also* pasta)

    marinara ................. 194

spatula ..................... 28

speck ...................... 206

spice(s)

    bag.................. 44, 46-53

    cooking with.........88, 92, 98

    Spice-kissed applesauce ..... 238

spice bag................. 44, 46-53

Spicy scrambled egg breakfast burrito ........................... 108

Spicy peanut noodles .......... 197

spills .......... 32, 35, 43, 62, 63, 74

spinach ..................151, 233

spoon(s)

    measuring spoons........... 29

    MSR Alpine Spoon .......... 28

    wooden spoons ..........28, 64

spork .....................29, 64

spreads

    Guacamole ............... 134

INDEX   271

spreads (*continued*)

    Lemony garlic bean Spread... 135

staple ingredients ............ 34-44

stew (see soup)

stir-fry.................... 189-191

stool ........................ 33

storage (see food storage)

stove(s)

    about..................... 25

    advice .............. 71-76, 96

    fuel bottle (see fuel bottle)

    Whisperlite........... 25, 73, 96

strainer lid ................... 24

Strawberries in syrup.......... 247

substitutions............... 91, 125

summer salad, black bean....... 148

supper recipes ............ 162-235

sugar........................ 92

Sweet-spicy peanut noodles .... 197

syrup, Strawberries in.......... 247

Tangy lemon curd............. 251

thyme ...................... 52

Toad-in-the-hole (see eggs)

tomato(es), canned

    about..................... 63

    Chili con carne ............ 164

    Tomato soup.............. 176

tomato(es), fresh

    Fresh tomato salsa ......... 133

    in salad .................. 151

    preparing................. 81

    Tomato mozzarella calzone .. 229

    tomato and cucumber salad

    (*Salade Tunisienne*) .......... 147

tomato paste

    about..................... 39

    Chili con carne ............ 164

    Spaghetti marinara ......... 194

    Tomato soup.............. 176

Tomato soup ................ 176

tools ..................... 24-33

tortilla

    chips ......... 133, 134, 148, 155

    Spicy scrambled egg breakfast

    burrito................... 108

    Tyler's tortillas ............ 222

tuna

    Camper's tuna casserole..... 202

    *Salade Tunisienne* .......... 147

Tunisian tomato-cucumber salad. 147

turnover(s)

    Cherry chocolate turnovers . 242

    filling options ............. 245

Tyler's favorites

    Our very favorite cheesy garlic

    pasta ................. 186-188

    Tyler's dumplings........... 175

    Tyler's fried potatoes ....... 208

    Tyler's grilled cheese........ 183

    Tyler's tortillas ............ 222

ultra-heat treated (UHT) milk.... 41

utensils .................. 28, 64

UV light water purifier ......... 32

vanilla extract

    about.................. 47, 52

    Banana nut oatmeal ........ 114

    Browned butter crepes .. 123-125

    Chocolate fudge oat cookies . 256

French toast . . . . . . . . . . . . . . 116
veganism . . . . . . . . . . . . . . . . . . . . 97
vegetable(s) (see also specific vegetables)
- as snacks . . . . . . . . . . . . . . . . . 155
- Garlicky green beans . . . . . . . 218
- Mixed salad . . . . . . . . . . . . . . 151
- peeler . . . . . . . . . . . . . . . . . . 29, 63
- Zucchini feta fritters . . . . . . . . 214
- Rice noodles with stir-fried broccoli and onion . . . . . . 189-191
- *Salade Tunisienne* (Tunisian tomato and cucumber Salad) . . . . . . . . 147

vegetarianism . . . . . . . . . . . . . . . . 97
Vinaigrette dressing . . . . . . . . . . . 151
vinegar (see also acidity)
- about . . . . . . . . . . . . . . . . . . . . 40
- *Salade Tunisienne* (Tunisian tomato and cucumber Salad) . . . . . . . . 147
- Vinaigrette dressing . . . . . . . . 151

Walkstool . . . . . . . . . . . . . . . . . . . 33
washing (see dishwashing)
water
- advice . . . . . . . . . . . . . . . . . 71, 84
- carrying . . . . . . . . . . . . . . . . . . 84
- for dishwashing . . . . . . . . . . 86-87
- for pasta . . . . . . . . . . . . . . . . 185
- filtration . . . . . . . . . . . . . . . . . 32
- purification . . . . . . . . . . . . . . . 32
- where to find . . . . . . . . . . . 85-86

waterproof basin
- Ortlieb folding bowl . . . . . . . . 32

Whisperlite . . . . . . . . . . . . . 25, 73, 96
wild foods (see Foraging)

wind screen . . . . . . . . . . . . . . . 25, 64
winging it . . . . . . . . . . . . . . . . . 88-93
X-plates, Sea to Summit . . . . . . . . . 28
yogurt . . . . . . . . . . . . . . . . . . . . . 126
zucchini
- preparing . . . . . . . . . . . . . . . . . 81
- Feta fritters . . . . . . . . . . . . . . 214

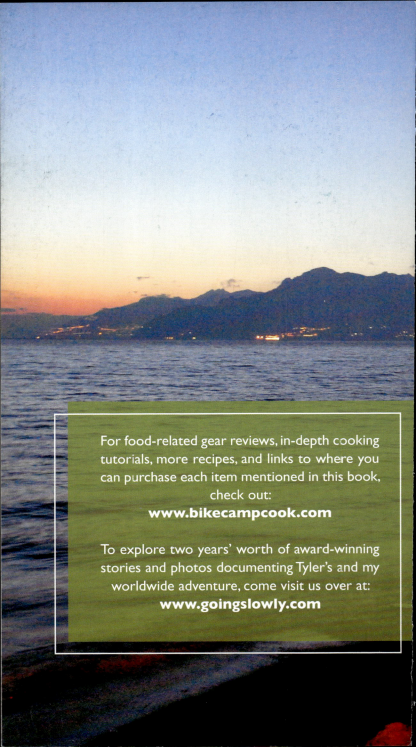

For food-related gear reviews, in-depth cooking tutorials, more recipes, and links to where you can purchase each item mentioned in this book, check out:
**www.bikecampcook.com**

To explore two years' worth of award-winning stories and photos documenting Tyler's and my worldwide adventure, come visit us over at:
**www.goingslowly.com**

Our tent, pitched for free on the Amalfi coast of Italy

# Recipe Notes

# Recipe Notes